What the Blind Man Saw

To Amy!
from one preacher
to another,
with love + best wishes,

John Killinger

What the Blind Man Saw

Sermons Based on Hidden Mark

JOHN KILLINGER

Parson's Porch Books   Cleveland, Tennessee

2010

Parson's Porch Books
121 Holly Trail, NW
Cleveland, Tennessee 37311

Unless otherwise noted, all scripture references are to the Revised
Standard Version, copyright Thomas Nelson Co., 1988.

To order additional copies of this book, contact:

Parson's Porch Books
1-423-475-7308
www.parsonsporch.com

Cover design: Eric Killinger
Cover art: Cartoon for stained glass window, *Jesus Stills the Storm*, Marble Collegiate
Church, New York City. Ink and charcoal on paper, 2002, Debora Coombs, artist.
Used by permission of the artist.

Contents

Foreword

The senior editor of a major religious publishing house to whom I first sent the manuscript of *Hidden Mark* told me he would be happy to publish it if I would rewrite it for a scholarly audience. I refused, explaining that the Gospel of Mark was intended for a general audience and I would like my book to appeal to a similar audience. I feel the same about this book, a collection of sermons based on the interpretations in *Hidden Mark*. It too is intended for everybody—laity, ministers, and even academics.

Some preachers, I realize, may wish to employ the sermons in their own pulpits, and I give them my blessing to do so, provided they illustrate them with stories from their own experience and not simply adopt mine as their own. One of the great Scottish pulpiteers—I believe it was old Alexander Whyte—advised his preaching students to stick their forks into the stew and whatever came up on them was theirs to use as they liked. The important thing is to *rethink* the sermons one uses, so that one speaks from the inside of the sermon and not merely from the outside, like a poacher.

I look upon this book as a kind of midrash or commentary on *Hidden Mark*, showing how certain ideas or concepts in that book can be fleshed out in the actual preaching of the gospel. I hope it will be as helpful to laity as to clergy, for many lay people are as literate as their pastors and as eager to gain meaningful insights into the faith of early Christianity. They will not be put off, I hope, by my suggestion that the Gospel of Mark was probably written from the perspective of Christian Gnosticism instead of the blander orthodoxy prevailing in the ecclesiastical politics of the second and third centuries.

Gnosticism, it should be explained, was widespread in the Greco-Roman world, and was especially rife among the so-called mystery cults, which maintained strict secrecy about their rites and beliefs. It was natural, given such an environment, that early Christianity should absorb some of its ways and ideas, which it did especially in North Africa, where it is generally held that Mark lived after Simon Peter's death in Rome. The basic premise of Gnosticism was that salvation belongs to those who have achieved a certain *gnosis* or knowledge of the god they worship. And it usually followed Plato's belief that the mind or spirit is superior to the body, leading to a certain disdain for the flesh.

When I began writing *Hidden Mark*, I did so without any thought of Mark's being a Gnostic document. But in the process of examining its literary patterns, I gradually realized that it was not only Gnostic but that its Gnosticism explained things about it that have long puzzled scholars—especially the so-called Messianic Secret (Jesus' bidding those he healed not to tell anyone), the pairing of feeding miracles (5,000 people on one occasion and 4,000 on another) and calming-of-the-sea stories (once when Jesus was in the boat and another time when he came walking through the storm at night), the slowness of the disciples to grasp what Jesus was about, the healing miracle that didn't "take" the first time (the blind man who saw "men like trees walking"), and the absence of a full-blown resurrection narrative at the end of the Gospel, which most scholars agree occurs at Mark 16:8.

Personally, I find my own faith greatly energized by this new understanding of a Gospel I have read all my life but did not fully appreciate until recently. I often found myself becoming very excited as I wrote these sermons, and wished I could preach them each Sunday to a congregation of my own, for I think the fresh interpretations will find great receptivity among most Christians.

Preachers will recognize what I am talking about. There is a well known saying among us that has to do with new information, a fresh twist on a familiar text, or a particularly illuminative or moving illustration. "That will preach!" we say with enthusiasm. I think many of the novel insights in *Hidden Mark* and this book of sermons will strike most preachers in this manner and make them eager to share the ideas with their congregations.

The Gnostics were certainly right about one thing—something with which I think even most evangelicals will readily agree—that all true religious experience is born of an encounter with mystery, with something that lies outside one's usual domain and puzzles or challenges the mind and heart to find a new level of understanding. This may be why Jesus said we must become as little children to enter the kingdom of God, and why the disciples, all grown men with their perceptions largely shaped, had such a difficult time reconciling what they encountered in Jesus with their usual way of organizing experience.

The same is still true for us today. We will not grow in our
spirits or in our faith until we are prepared to receive Jesus himself as a mystery, as someone whose ways and sayings we have
not yet, even now, understood. At least that is what I have
found for myself.

JOHN KILLINGER

What the Blind Man Saw

Take It From The Beginning

Mark 1:1-34

The first words of any document are always important—of a letter to the editor or a note to an in-
amorata or a business letter or a newspaper editorial
or a short story or a novel. When I taught creative writing, I
sometimes asked my students to spend thirty minutes compos-
ing the most intriguing sentence they could contrive, one that
would compel the reader to want to read on.

I remember one of those sentences: "It began as a low rumble, like the sound of a distant freight train, and before he could
get out of bed it had struck in all its fury, blowing glass and de-
bris everywhere." Another was: "She had not noticed before,
but as she set her tea cup down on the oil cloth she felt a definite twinge along her right arm, beginning just above the elbow
and running into the hollow beneath her shoulder."

The first words of the Gospel of Mark may appear somewhat tame beside these well crafted sentences. They don't grasp
us by the collar and scream at us, "You must read this!" In fact,
they seem rather bland, considering the dynamic nature of the
material that is to follow. Bland and understated.

But are they?

For a modern novel, maybe. But not for an important document like the earliest Gospel we have.

Arche tou euangelion Iesou Christou. "The beginning of the good news of Jesus Christ." Didn't Mark think we knew it was the beginning? It certainly wasn't the middle or the end. What else could it be?

But wait! How did the Hebrew Bible begin? "In the beginning." Before anything else—even before the world was made.

Maybe Mark was aware of that when he started his Gospel, and wanted to link what was beginning with Jesus to what had begun in the very origin of time itself. John would start his Gospel in much the same way, probably with the same connection in mind: "In the beginning was the Word."

There is something sacred about beginnings, isn't there? The beginning of life at birth. A baby's first steps. The beginning of school. The beginning of a new job. The beginning of a marriage. The beginning of anything big and important. We have ribbon-cuttings to celebrate the opening of a new building and we crack champagne bottles across the bows of ships before their maiden voyages.

We honor beginnings. We honor endings too, but there is something mysterious about beginnings, for the journeys are yet to be made, the adventures yet to come. There is hope and promise in the beginning. There are stirrings and excitement.

What did the famed anthropologist Loren Eiseley call the story of his becoming a naturalist—*The Immense Journey?* All journeys seem immense at the start, don't they? As Cicero said, each begins with a single step. The faltering step of a child just learning to walk. The hesitant step of a child leaving home. The confident step of a young professional at his or her first job. The weary step of the parent who has presided over the growth of children. The slowing, uncertain step of the older adult. The immense journey that begins slowly, simply, with determination.

And for Mark, *the beginning of good news.*

Most of his readers had not enjoyed a lot of good news. They had grown up in an occupied land and paid taxes to a foreign government. They were poor and largely illiterate. They lived and died as slaves. Marriage was usually for convenience and not for love. Life was hard and earnest. Meals were uncertain. Sickness often meant death. So good news was—well, unexpected, to say the least. Nobody would have predicted it. And, because it wasn't expected, nobody would have complained if it hadn't come.

But it wasn't mere good news. It was attached to a person. It was a kind of biography. It was *the beginning of the good news of Jesus Christ.*

Albert Einstein, says Matthew Fox in the prologue to *The Coming of the Cosmic Christ,* was once asked, "What is the most important question you can ask in life?" His answer was: "Is the universe a friendly place or not?" In Jesus' time, says Fox, the question was similar: "Are the angels friend or foe?" People then didn't think as secularly as Einstein. For them, the angels were the driving forces behind everything. Therefore they wanted to know if the angels were friendly to them.

The early Christian answer to their question, says Fox, was very definite: "Jesus represented the smiling face of God, the benignity of the universe and all its powers including the invisible angels. All the early hymns to the Cosmic Christ composed by first-century Christians celebrate the power of Jesus Christ over thrones, dominations and angels."[1]

1. Matthew Fox, *The Coming of the Cosmic Christ* (Harper & Row, 1988), p. 1.

That's why the story of Jesus was called good news. God was on their side. The angels cared about what happened to them. So who could possibly be against them?

Some people were, of course. The world wasn't overly friendly. Crooks and murderers and dishonest politicians abounded. Sickness and injuries took their toll. Poverty had the same unbearable odor it has today. In fact, everything was pretty much as it is today—as we are.

Mark's point was that the good news was about Jesus. God made manifest in the flesh. God touching and healing people. God feeding the masses. God struggling with and overthrowing evil. God overcoming death itself.

That *was* good news!

Jesus was the fulfillment of a promise made by the radical prophet John, the baptizer who immersed people in the Jordan when they repented of their sins, the promise that one greater than himself was coming. And after Jesus was baptized by John, the Spirit led him into the wilderness for forty days of spiritual warfare, after which "the angels waited on him."[2]

A good sign: the angels were on his side.

Then John was arrested and Jesus went into Galilee "proclaiming the good news of God, and saying, 'The time is fulfilled, and the kingdom of God has come near; repent, and believe in the good news.'"[3] He enlisted the help of some fishermen—not scribes and Pharisees from Jerusalem, who were part of the institutional bureaucracy, but simple laborers with boats—and together they went to Capernaum, a fishing center on the Sea of Galilee, and he began his ministry of teaching.

There he entered the synagogue and spoke with such wisdom that people "were astounded at his teaching, for he taught

2. Mark 1:13
3. Mark 1:15

them as one having authority, not as one of the scribes."⁴ But there was an enemy there—a man with an unclean spirit, as the Bible puts it—and he began to rail against Jesus, who he said had come to destroy them.

Jesus' first miracle in the Gospel of Mark is the casting out of a demon from this man who was objecting to his ministry—and the people were more impressed than ever because they knew he acted with divine power.

When he and his followers left the synagogue, they went to the house of Simon Peter and Andrew, where Peter's wife's mother was in bed with a fever. Jesus' second miracle was banishing her fever and setting her back on her feet.

Such small beginnings: one demon cast out, and one sick woman healed.

But then his ministry began in earnest. After sundown, people began bringing their sick and demon-possessed to him, "and the whole city gathered around the door."⁵ Imagine! The whole city gathered around a single house where two fishermen lived with their families!

There is an interesting note at this point. Mark says the demons knew who he was and he would not permit them to speak, lest they tell everyone who he was. It is the first instance of the Messianic Secret, of Jesus' desire for anonymity and his request that there be no real announcement of his heavenly identity.

So we have the beginning of Jesus' ministry.

Not wild and splashy at first. Quiet and low key.

But it quickly escalated. A whole city gathered around the house where he healed people.

And this, says Mark, was the beginning—the starting

---

4. Mark 1:22
5. Mark 1:33

point—the kick-off—the prologue to a life so grand, so expansive, so filled with magic and conflict that we can't begin to imagine it.

Except for what Mark tells us.

Except for all the stories to come—multiple healings, conflicts with institutional religion, the appointment of twelve disciples, the feeding of multitudes, calming the sea when the disciples were about to perish, raising the dead, crossing borders to minister to Gentiles, transfiguration in the mountains, the incredible teachings, conflict in the Holy City, death on a cross, and news of his resurrection.

What a story it was! What a journey he had!

And all from a simple beginning.

His business with us usually begins simply too, doesn't it? No great fanfare. No sudden, prodigious upheaval. Only a notion. Or something somebody said. Or a fragment of a dream remembered. Or a book. Or a prayer. Or the look on someone's face. Or the sound and words of a hymn.

I am haunted by Anne Lamott's description of her conversion. She wanted nothing to do with Jesus. Sometimes she stopped at a battered little Presbyterian church on the edge of Sausalito and listened to the singing, but she always left before the sermon. She was pregnant, but didn't want to marry the father, so she had an abortion. Afterward, she was on her houseboat in the harbor, drinking and popping pills, when she began to bleed heavily. She thought of calling the doctor but was afraid. After several hours, the bleeding stopped. She got into bed, too wild and shaky to have another drink or take a sleeping pill. She lit a cigarette and turned off the light.

Then she says:

After a while, as I lay there, I became aware of someone with me, hunkered down in the corner, and I just assumed it was my father, whose presence I had felt over the years when I was frightened and alone. The feeling was so strong that I actually turned on the light for a moment to make sure no one was there—of course, there wasn't. But after a while, in the dark again, I knew beyond any doubt that it was Jesus. I felt him as surely as I feel my dog lying nearby as I write this.[6]

She was appalled. What would her friends think of her if she became a Christian? She didn't think she could bear it. She turned toward the wall and said aloud, "I would rather die."

But she could feel him there in the darkness, hunkered down and watching her with patience and love. She squinched her eyes, trying to see him, but of course she couldn't, because it wasn't her eyes she was seeing him with.

Finally she fell asleep, and in the morning he was gone.

But she began to sense him following her, like a little cat that paused when she paused and walked on when she did. She couldn't get rid of it. It wanted her to pick it up and take it home and give it some milk, but she had had experience with cats and knew you can't get rid of them once you do that, so she tried to ignore it.

On Sunday she returned to the little church for the singing. But she was so hung-over that she remained in her seat for the sermon, which she found ridiculous and unbelievable, as if the preacher were trying to convince everybody of the existence of extraterrestrials. The last song got to her, though. She began to

6. Anne Lamott, *Traveling Mercies: Some Thoughts on Faith* (Pantheon, 1999), p. 49.

cry, and left before the benediction. She raced home, aware that the little cat was running along at her heels. She walked down the dock past the other houseboats and unlocked the door of hers. Then, she says, she uttered a curse word and said she quit. Then she took a long deep breath and said out loud, "All right. You can come in."[7]

This, she says, was her "beautiful moment of conversion."

Mark, I think, would have liked her story. He would have understood this beginning, because he understood that this was the kind of effect Jesus had on people.

That's why he called it good news.

7. Ibid., p. 50.

Hunting for Jesus

Mark 1:35-39

Have you ever thought about the word *hunting* and how curious it is? It comes from an Old English word, *huntian*, and then the Middle English word *hunten*. Its primary meaning was to pursue a quarry of some kind, either for sport or for meat. Then it was co-opted for use in less serious pursuits, such as hunting for an object one had misplaced or hunting for flowers or hunting for a person one knew. Now we use it quite indiscriminately. "I'm hunting for a red blouse," says a friend in a department store, or "I'm hunting for the ingredients for a new recipe I want to try."

But imagine hunting for *Jesus*. Have you ever thought of doing that? We usually think of Jesus as the hunter, not the hunted. We cite Francis Thompson's famous poem, "The Hound of Heaven":

> *I fled Him, down the nights and down the days;*
> *I fled Him, down the arches of the years;*
> *I fled Him, down the labyrinthine ways*
> *Of my own mind, and in the midst of tears*
> *I hid from him, and under running laughter.*

Hunting *him* is quite another thing. But it is what Mark says the disciples were doing.

They had not been with him long, if the swiftness with which Mark covers this ground is any indication. Mark touches on the salient parts of the early narrative about Christ—the prophetic ministry of John the Baptist, Jesus' coming to him to be baptized in the River Jordan, his being driven into the wilderness for testing (not *led*, in Mark's account, but *driven*), his calling of the first disciples (Peter and Andrew, James and John), his appearance at the synagogue in Capernaum (where he was rejected), and then his teaching and healing of the masses as "the whole city was gathered around the door."[1]

Mark doesn't dawdle in his narrative; he paints with broad, swift strokes.

Then he informs us that Jesus arose the next morning while it was still dark and went out to pray. Apparently it took the disciples a while to find him, because when they did, they said, "Everyone is searching for you."[2]

And what did Jesus say?

He had learned something in his prayer time—had received his orders from the Father. "Let us go on to the neighboring towns," he said, "so that I may proclaim the message there also; for that is what I came out to do."[3]

And that is what he did. What *they* did, for the die was cast and the disciples were swept up in his mission.

We could let it go at that. They hunted for Jesus, they found him, he told them what they must do, and they did it.

Or we could ask, Did Mark have something rather more significant in mind? Something more penetrating, even symbolic, in the phrase, they "hunted for him"? The Greek word

1. Mark 1:33.
2. Mark 1.37.
3. Mark 1:38.

employed in the Gospel is *katadioko*, which can be translated "they *tracked* him" or "they *pursued him relentlessly*."

We don't wish to invite scrutiny where the text doesn't warrant it. But perhaps, in light of what we now know about the Gospel of Mark and its Gnostic propensity for mystery and depths of meaning, it does seem possible that Mark was suggesting something that in the days of our simpler understanding of his narrative we would have passed over more lightly, without questioning.

They were hunting for Jesus.

Isn't that precisely what Mark is doing in the whole of his Gospel? He is ferreting out Jesus and the meaning of Jesus. In the raucous, populous, and often confusing world of early Christianity and its spread, Mark was hunting for the real Jesus, for an understanding of his life and death and resurrection that would be true and convincing for his readers.

We can understand this, can't we? How many books, especially mystery stories, begin with a detective committed to unraveling the truth about a situation, to solving a puzzle or conundrum, to arriving at a point of discovery where the reader himself or herself, along with the detective, becomes completely absorbed and enlightened?

One of the first books I ever owned, when I was perhaps thirteen or fourteen, was Dale Carnegie's *Lincoln the Unknown*. In the introduction Carnegie, also the author of the famous *How to Win Friends and Influence People*, told how he had first been awakened to the mystery of Abraham Lincoln's life by a series of articles in a London newspaper, and how that had led him to the British Museum, where he read many books about President Lincoln. He had begun writing his book then, but

later tore up all the pages to start again. He moved to Spring-
field, Illinois, to walk the very streets that Lincoln walked as a
young man, and lived among the kind of people Lincoln would
have known, so that he could better understand the personality
and thinking of the illustrious president.

Isn't this what Mark was about in his Gospel? It is possible
that he was the John Mark of the scriptures, so that he knew
Jesus personally. We can't know for sure. But whether he actually knew Jesus or not, he was a practicing Christian whose life
had been totally electrified and reordered by the living Christ,
and as such he was determined to lead his readers on a hunt
for Jesus, on a mental and emotional trek that would unearth
the deeper meaning of the Lord's existence and thus make it
possible for others who had never met him to effect nevertheless a kind of meeting with him, a *rapprochement* that would
change their lives as Mark's had been changed.

The disciples—especially Peter, Andrew, James, and
John—would be hunting for him throughout the narrative of
Mark's Gospel, as would others. But the real Jesus would prove
elusive. They would think they knew him, that they had hunted
him down, and then he would elude them, would rise above
their understanding with some new saying, some new action,
that would completely baffle them and make them wonder if
they would ever truly know him. He would often chide them
for their slowness of wit, their incapacity for apprehending the
truth of his presence. He would tell them they didn't have
enough faith. He would accuse them of being asleep, of being
indifferent to what was transpiring before their very eyes.

So their hunt would continue.

It would drag on and on and on, even for years during

which they dogged his steps and were present for many of his great pronouncements and extraordinary miracles. Yet, even at the end of the Gospel, they would still not understand, would still seem doltish and thick-headed and hard of seeing and hearing. They would flee before his captors, and Simon Peter would deny that he had even known the man. The women who came to the tomb would run away in fright, still unprepared for the mystery of his resurrection.

But in the hunting, the probing, the searching, there would be cracks and crevices where the mystery would ooze out like fog, creating an atmosphere where readers hundreds and thousands of years later could still feel a sense of his transcendent presence.

He would always be elusive, but in the search for him many of us would become caught up in that presence and inducted into his service.

Frederick Buechner, in *The Sacred Journey*, describes the process without speaking of it directly. Even in our most humdrum days, he says, God addresses us in mysterious ways. How does it happen? Buechner was writing his book on an ordinary summer's day. Outside, he could hear the twitter of swallows swooping in and out of the eaves of the barn. Several rooms away, in another part of the old farm house, some men were doing some carpentry work. He could hear the low rumble of their voices, the muted sound of their hammers, and the uneven lengths of silence in between. In the distance, a rooster crowed, even though it was long after sunup.

As Buechner wrote, half-listening to the sounds, the various noises began to assume harmonies and rhythms in his mind, until he began to think he was hearing the sounds of his own life speaking to him. The music of them was fresh and unique and appealing. He had no idea what it meant, or what his life was telling him.

> What does the song of a swallow mean? What is the muffled sound of a hammer trying to tell? And yet as I listened to those sounds, and listened with something more than just my hearing, I was moved by their inexpressible eloquence and suggestiveness, by the sense I had that they were a music rising up out of the mystery of not just my life, but of life itself. In much the same way, that is what I mean by saying that God speaks into or out of the thick of our days.[4]

So it is with Mark's Gospel. There are probably notes and sounds in it that were strange and unknown even to him. Yet he knew, as he crafted his narrative, that God would use them to seduce the senses of his readers, to call them away from their ordinary lives and into the magic and miracle of the man about whom he was writing. Just as God takes the strange scribblings of a Bach or a Mozart and converts them into an incredibly beautiful sonata, so he takes Mark's attempts at painting a portrait of Jesus and uses them to beguile the souls who read the Gospel, to entrance them to the point of surrendering to a higher power, of allowing their own lives to be overmastered by the deity.

It is all still a mystery—how this can be, who Jesus actually was, what he really said and did, and what meaning it holds for us. But it is so rich and intriguing a mystery that we cannot help joining in the search for Jesus, hunting for him just as the

4. Frederick Buechner, *The Sacred Journey* (Harper & Row, 1982), p. 3.

disciples did, and trying to piece together for our own time and understanding a portrait of the remarkable servant of God that prompted such a portrait of him in Mark's day.

Morton Smith was right to say, in his book *Jesus the Magician*, that trying to find the real Jesus is like trying in atomic physics to locate a submicroscopic particle and determine its charge.[5] We can't see the particle by itself, but we can trace its lines of motion by the other particles it has set in motion. There is no way we shall ever produce a completely accurate portrait of Jesus, or even one so satisfyingly accurate that we are able to say, "There he is; now set your compass by him."

Even Mark himself said of the Gospel he was undertaking to write that it was only "the *beginning* of the good news of Jesus Christ, the Son of God."[6]

But each of us is able, if we are determined to search him out, to hunt for him as the disciples did and as Mark did, to discover enough evidence of his presence, enough lines of his effects on other people and on the world at large, to feel our own lives being galvanized by him, and to surrender to him and his mission to the world as ecstatically as the early disciples did.

Kathleen Norris, in *Dakota: A Spiritual Geography*, says that "Like Jacob's angel, the region requires that you wrestle with it before it bestows a blessing."[7] The same can be said about hunting Jesus. We must delve, we must seek, we must turn over many leaves and stones in an effort to find him for ourselves, before we receive the blessing.

And when we have done it—when we have truly searched as Mark and the other Gospel writers did—we shall have the blessing, and have it abundantly.

I know, for I have had it.

---

5. Morton Smith, *Jesus the Magician* (Harper & Row, 1978), p. 7.
6. Mark 1:1.
7. Kathleen Norris, *Dakota: A Spiritual Geography* (Houghton Mifflin, 1993), p. 1.

Don't Tell Anyone What God Has Done for You

Mark 1:40-45

This is indeed strange, isn't it? "See that you say nothing to anyone."[1] Don't tell what has happened to you. Don't shine the spotlight on Jesus, who gave you a miracle in your life. It isn't to be talked about. Keep it out of the newspapers and off the TV. Mum's the word!

Not only does it go against human nature, which is to run out and shout the news from the housetops, but it goes against all our teachings and instincts as Christians, that we are to bear witness to what God has done for us, even to the end of the earth!

We understand why the leper disobeyed. Imagine what a bind Jesus' words put him in. Here was a man so ravaged by the insidious power of leprosy that he had probably lost fingers and toes to the disease, perhaps even a foot or a leg. He had lived for years with this enemy in his own body, this evil force that was daily destroying who he was. He was banned from all normal human contacts—worship in the synagogue, fraternization in the village square, even the comfort of a family. The disease was eating away at his very soul, at everything that made him human and provided him with joy.

1. Mark 1:44.

Imagine yourself in his condition, and then imagine that you had encountered Jesus and been made whole. Jesus told him to go to the priest and show himself, for that was the way back into society, for the priest to validate that there had been a healing and he was once more fit for cohabiting with others in the community. Wouldn't you have been so overjoyed that you would have told the news just as he did?

Reynolds Price, the writing teacher at Duke University, tells in his book *A Whole New Life* of the complete debilitation of his life when he was crippled by multiple sclerosis and a large tumor growing in his spine. Normally healthy and robust, he was suddenly stricken and rendered helpless by this mysterious mass on his central nervous system. Consultations with doctors led to surgery, weeks in the hospital, rehabilitation exercises, radiation therapy, and being suspended somewhere between hope and despair.

Then came his remarkable dream.

He had visited the Sea of Galilee on two occasions, and now that was where his dream was set. He dreamed that he had just awakened in the early morning and there were men around him on the ground sleeping in their tunics. He realized without being told that they were Jesus and his twelve disciples. One of them stirred and rose. It was Jesus himself. Jesus approached him and silently motioned for him to follow. Price rose, removed all his clothing, and followed as Jesus walked into the lake. They waded out about twenty feet and stood waist-deep in the cool water. Price says he was both present in his body and yet also outside and above it, so that he could see the purple dye on his back, the tattoo the radiologists had made so they could pinpoint their radiation of his affected areas.

Jesus, he said, raised handfuls of water and let them fall onto his back, trickling down across the puckered scar of his recent operation. The Lord spoke only once. "Your sins are forgiven," he said. Then he turned and waded back to shore, through with his work on Price. Price followed, eager to learn more. It wasn't his sins he was worried about, he said; it was his tumor.

"Am I also cured?" he asked.

Jesus turned and looked at him, unsmiling. "That too," he said, leaving the water and climbing up the bank.

Then Price awoke, back in his own bed.

Yet he could not separate himself from the reality of what he had experienced, and continued to believe that somehow, in an unfathomable mystery, the dream was "an external gift, however brief, of an alternate time and space in which to live through a crucial act."[2]

He needed such a gift, for his way was still very difficult, fraught by dozens of radiation treatments that destroyed good cells with bad and kept him weak and dependent on others for months to come.

Price makes a point of the fact that a few years earlier, in the 1970s, he had spent months making his own translation of the Gospel of Mark from the Greek into modern English. He suspects that this had something to do with his having the dream about Jesus at the Sea of Galilee. His mind and soul were steeped in the picture of Jesus as healer and caster-out of demons. He made drawing after drawing of what he had experienced—Christ pouring the water on his back and giving him forgiveness.

But did he hesitate to tell? Did Jesus' forbidding the leper

2. Reynolds Price, *A Whole New Life* (Plume/Penguin, 1995), pp. 43-44.

to talk about his restoration enter Price's mind at all? Apparently not, for he put it in his book for all to read and know about. It was the equivalent, or more, of shouting the news from the housetop!

We are all eager to give God or Christ the credit when we have been healed of something as grave as leprosy or a tumor on the spine. It is a natural reaction. Not to tell would seem— well, churlish at worst and unmannerly at best.

Then why did Jesus insist on such a veil of secrecy for what he did? Because he had enough crowds about him, enough poor souls to heal, without anybody's spreading the word? Perhaps that was a factor. He was certainly busy, with barely a moment to get alone with his Father in prayer.

But in Mark's view there was apparently more, and his reason does not come quickly to our attention because for centuries we have missed one important fact about his Gospel, that it was written from a gnostic perspective. We don't know a lot about the Gnostics. Certainly more than our fathers and mothers did a generation or two before our own. The invaluable discovery of the so-called Nag Hammadi Library on the banks of the Nile River in 1945 has greatly enriched our knowledge at this point, for it was full of old manuscripts written by Gnostics and then hidden in a water-tight jar because the orthodox Christians of the second century had declared Gnosticism a heresy and probably excommunicated those who openly admitted to being of that persuasion. Yet, in spite of the discovery, we still know very little.

What we do know is that the Gnostics were probably influenced in their practices by the so-called mystery religions of the Roman Empire, and that one of the characteristic traits of those religions was a tendency to keep all things secret from the outside world. Thus their adherents met in secret and swore to keep their rites and teachings hidden from everybody else. This was partly owing to their fear of persecution by others and partly owing to how highly they valued the knowledge they possessed, so that they did not wish it to be diluted or misunderstood by the public at large.

In *Hidden Mark*, I have gone at some length into my reasons for conjecturing that Mark is actually more Gnostic than was suspected. At the core of these reasons is my belief that the two calming-of-the-sea stories in Mark 4 and Mark 6 are in fact not mere miracle stories—Jesus extended his hands and ordered a raging sea to become docile—but are instead Mark's picture of the resurrected Christ imposing peace on the troubled environment of a beleaguered early church. For years, scholars have puzzled over the way the original Gospel ends, in chapter 16, with the account of the women who came to the tomb, discovered that the body of Jesus was missing, were told by an angel to go and tell the others that Christ was raised, and went away and said nothing because they were afraid. But this apparently truncated ending makes perfect sense if we take the calming-of-the-sea stories as resurrection accounts.

It is Mark's way of saying that the resurrection is a mystery too deep for human understanding and should not be confined to the kind of fairy-tale resurrection invoked by the other Gospel writers. It is a spiritual truth—a secret given to true believers—and does not depend in any way on human reason or on a verifiable resuscitation of the actual body of Jesus. Gnostic Christians were leery of a less spiritual interpretation of what occurred, the one involving a literal physical resurrection.

Now, as I indicated, it was also characteristic of Gnostic Christians that, like the adherents of Greco-Roman mystery cults, they tried to preserve as their own private mysteries the more intimate details of Jesus' life and ministry, and to share these as part of their ritual life together, not to bruit them abroad like common gossip. It was perfectly natural to them, therefore, that Jesus himself would not be an overly public persona, healing people of their illnesses and infirmities and then using those healings as public-relations events to make his name better known to the masses. Instead, they imagined he would be as reverent of the mysteries involving healing and restoration as they, and would therefore caution those who experienced divine intervention in their illnesses and infirmities to say nothing about what had occurred to them except perhaps within the cultic community itself.

A personal experience has helped me to understand this kind of reticence in the face of such mysteries. Several years ago, I had some serious lung surgery at a hospital in Detroit. I came through the operation with flying colors. But four days later a shower of emboli from blood clots in my legs attacked my lungs and endangered my life. As evening fell and my wife, son, and daughter-in-law were compelled to leave the ICU where I was resting and return to their motel, they stopped in the hospital chapel to have a prayer for my recovery. They were kneeling near the front of the chapel. When my wife finished praying, she opened her eyes and lifted her head in time to see a strange white apparition emerge from the carved wooden reredos in the chancel and waft its way up the short aisle and through the back door. Noticing that our son had also finished praying, she asked if he had seen anything.

"Yes," he said. "It was something white, and it went up the aisle. Do you think it was the angel of death?"

"No," said my wife. "It was Gabriel, the angel John saw once when he was a boy of sixteen. He's going to be all right."

Now, this occurrence was very important to my wife and son, and, after they told it to me, to me as well. Like Reynolds Price's dream, it became part of my healing, an inseparable part of it. But it was so important, so deeply meaningful, that it was not something we rushed out to tell others about, for to have done so would have inexplicably cheapened the event, would have made it seem less real than it was to all of us. Because we cherished it and the meaning it evoked, we wanted to preserve it for a while as ours and ours alone, to tell it only to one another and not to a host of other people.

I believe the semantics of this occasion and how we felt about it are similar to those in Mark's Gospel, where, on several occasions throughout the narrative, people are cautioned not to speak to others about what Christ has done for them, but to quietly rejoin society as if nothing transcendent had actually taken place. Thus the leper in our text was instructed to show himself to the priest for validation of his cure, but otherwise to maintain a discrete silence about it.

What it says to me is that Mark had an acute sensitivity to the subtle relationship between an external event—say, the healing of a leper—and the internal appropriation of that event by the person to whom it happened. What God does in the realm of a human world, in other words, is so special, so sacred, that one does not easily or glibly speak of it to others. It is something to be treasured in one's heart, to be held to one's breast as if it were a precious jewel continuing to give hope and sustenance to what is within the breast. A real miracle is very difficult to speak of, for it loses some of its transcendent power in the telling of it.

Scholars have become accustomed to calling Jesus' caution toward reticence the Messianic Secret, as if Jesus had some ulterior or unspoken reason for not wishing people to hear about his extraordinary miracles. To me, this is inadequate as an explanation. I believe it has far less to do with the privacy of the Messiah himself than it does with his (and Mark's) preternatural sensitivity to the divine-human transaction occurring in the individuals being restored to wholeness. To tell would be to vitiate that transaction. To remain silent would be to cultivate the occurrence, to preserve it in its pristine power and beauty.

Some things, in other words, are too precious and important for speech. They should be caressed and nurtured and preserved in transcendent silence, so that their value glows with otherworldly incandescence and continues its work of converting the heart to its fullest possibilities.

I am not sure if it is a good comparison, but years ago I read in a book about bibliophiles of a certain lover of books in the days when their pages were not cut at the printers who, whenever he received a new book in the post, carefully cut open the pages while holding the volume upside down, so that he would not absorb too much of the contents while doing so. That is the kind of sensitivity I have been attempting to describe, only with regard to one's personal healing and restoration to wholeness.

It was and is, I believe, part of Mark's own sensitiveness to the work of the Spirit that was being conducted through Jesus. As much as he believed the gospel was for everyone and wanted it to be known and claimed by people far and wide, he did not wish it to become common or vulgar in any sense. He would have deplored the kind of pandering evangelism we see on every hand today, and would have denied that it had anything to do with the real spirit of Christ, which was a spirit of vibrancy and holiness evoked by the very presence of God in our midst.

Perhaps we all need to pray more and speak less.

Which Comes First,
the People or the Law?

Mark 2:1-12

In Sarah Orne Jewett's quaint masterpiece *The Country of the Pointed Firs*, Maine's great regional writer describes the home of a retired sea captain. Of particular interest are a number of painted wooden markers placed haphazardly around the yard of his house. An orderly, thoughtful man, says Ms. Jewett, the captain erected these markers over the spots where rocks lay just beneath the surface in order to warn anyone plowing the ground that their plow would almost certainly hang up there.

When I read about that thoughtful arrangement, I decided it was an apt metaphor for the laws God gave to the Israelites. They were not intended as oppressive legal restrictions, but as markers to warn people that danger lay beneath the surface at particular points of their existence. Killing, stealing, coveting a neighbor's wife, dishonoring parents all threatened to disrupt individuals' lives and tear apart the social fabric of the nation as a whole. So God was saying, with each commandment, there is trouble here: avoid it!

But there are some people who never meet a law or a boundary that they don't fall in love with. In fact, they adore legal restrictions so much that they actually dote on them. They want more and more of them. They meditate on ways to extrapolate additional restrictions from the ones they already have. They are like an old goat my family once owned that had an absolute penchant for getting tangled up in wire of any kind. She seemed to actively seek out old pieces of fencing she could get embroiled in, and would lie down and become entangled in them as if someone had trussed her up.

By the time of Jesus, several hundred years after God had given the commandments to Moses, the body of Jewish laws had grown so complex and restrictive that there were people called scribes who did nothing but study it and elaborate on it most of their lives. The scribes were a society of old goats who loved the fencing people got tangled up in, and most of them liked nothing better than finding someone who was in flagrant violation of a law and insisting on that person's punishment. And the closer one got to Jerusalem, the capital of the Holy Land, the thicker the scribes were, and the more eagle-eyed to spot the minutest infractions of the law.

Jesus, on the other hand, was a pragmatist. He was from Galilee, a northern province where there were few scribes and people were more practical minded about legalities. To him the spirit of the law was more important than the letter of it. We know this from some of his teachings in the Sermon on the Mount: the person who has killed another in his heart is as guilty as if he had actually committed murder; the one who has lusted has in effect already succumbed to adultery; and so on. It was natural, as the scribes heard about Jesus' liberalism toward the law and began to infiltrate the crowds where he taught and healed, that they should mark him as a dangerous enemy to everything they stood for.

Mark had a good reason for setting this text near the beginning of his account of Jesus' life and ministry. (John did a similar thing in his Gospel by setting the story of the wedding at Cana of Galilee at the head of his narrative—John 2:1-11—for he wanted to emphasize that a transcendent power had arrived on the scene, changing the water of the old law into the wine of the new age.) Mark wanted to say to all his readers, "Here is a key thing about Jesus: he has compassion on people and will not permit unwarranted legal embellishments to discourage him from exercising that compassion."

So he told this story about a paralyzed man whose friends wanted so badly to bring him to Jesus that they carried him onto the top of a house where Jesus was teaching crowds of people, removed the lath and plaster, and lowered the man through a hole right into the presence of the Master.

Seeing the extraordinary faith of the man's friends, says Mark, Jesus announced to the paralyzed man, "Son, your sins are forgiven."[1] (These were precisely the words Reynolds Price heard Jesus say in his dream, when what he actually wanted to hear was, "You are healed.") Immediately a buzz went around the room. Who was this strange figure who dared to defy the tradition that channeled all of God's forgiveness through the priests and their sacrifices in the temple?

"Ah," said Jesus, knowing at once what they were thinking, "why are you murmuring like that? It would be all right with you if I said, 'Stand up and walk,' wouldn't it? But when I forgive a man's sins, you throw up your hands in horror, for that is against your tradition. Which do you think is easier, to forgive sins or to say 'Take up your bed and walk'?"

So, says Mark, to prove that he was truly the Son of Man

1. Mark 2:5.

and had the authority to forgive sins, he demonstrated his power by commanding the man to take up his bed and go home, which the man immediately did, causing his critics to gasp in amazement and say, "We have never seen anything like this!"[2]

Almost instantly, as the verses that follow this story indicate, the scribes and Pharisees began to conspire against Jesus, for he was an obvious threat to their comfortable old system. His popularity actually rose to new levels, as great crowds continued to assemble wherever he went. But the line was drawn. His very existence was a troublesome annoyance to the elders who controlled Israel, and they would stop at nothing to eradicate him, for they were in love, not with God and God's people, but with their own positions of advantage.

Thus Mark made his point. He planted a huge torch in the ground at the beginning of his Gospel and its light would illumine the remainder of his story. It declared in no uncertain terms that Jesus loved people more than he cared for laws and traditions.

It wouldn't be an easy sell, even after the church became established, because there would always be Christians who felt more comfortable with laws and boundaries than with the pure Spirit of God. James—possibly Jesus' own brother and a leader in the early church—wrote an epistle that fairly crackled with *dos* and *don'ts*. "Whoever keeps the whole law but fails in one point," he admonished, "has become accountable for all of it."[3] And even the Apostle Paul, eloquent as he sometimes waxed about salvation by grace, could often sound like the old Pharisee he had once been, chiding fellow Christians for their transgressions.

2. Mark 2:12.
3. James 2:10.

But Mark was of a single mind on the matter: Jesus himself always put people above law or tradition. Chided because his disciples didn't fast the way John the Baptist's did, he replied, "The wedding guests cannot fast while the bridegroom is with them, can they?"[4] Berated for allowing his disciples to pluck and eat grains of wheat on the sabbath, he retorted, "The sabbath was made for humankind, and not humankind for the sabbath."[5] And again on a sabbath, faced by a man with a withered arm and surrounded by Pharisees eager to see if he would heal the man, he was grieved by their hardness of heart, says Mark, and commanded the man, "Stretch out your hand."[6]

There was never any question about where he stood. It was invariably with the little people who suffered and needed God's love and attention.

There may be something quite gnostic about this picture of Jesus. The Gnostics, who held to a duality of flesh and spirit, believed that the spirit always triumphs over flesh. Their Jesus, as God's transcendent presence in our midst, wouldn't care much for earthly laws and traditions. For him, God's love was a far greater reality than anything else, so he might easily appear to contemn the nit-picking of the scribes and Pharisees.

Pharisaism, as I have suggested, is natural to many people, and even in the best of times its strains have always been noticeable in the Christian community. A whole history of the church could be written in terms of the unresolved tension between its legalists and its free spirits. When the legalists are in the ascendancy, the church strikes others as mincing, negative, and forbidding; and when the free spirits are strongest, we most easily recall Jesus and the breath of fresh air he brought to religion in his day. But the tension is always there.

4. Mark 2:19
5. Mark 2:27.
6. Mark 3:5.

Ernst Käsemann, in *Jesus Means Freedom*, framed it in a little story of a small town in Holland whose dikes were in danger of collapsing because of a storm and rising tides. The elders of the village church were engaged in a debate about whether it was all right for their parishioners to work on the Lord's day to shore up the levees. During the debate, a young clergyman reminded them that Jesus once said that the sabbath was made for man, not man for the sabbath. "Aye," retorted one old elder, "I always did suspect that our Lord was a wee bit of a liberal!"[7]

This is what I mean about the ongoing tension.

But Mark wanted there to be no mistake about Jesus and where he stood. So he set this story at the very outset of the narrative, or near enough to it for it to hold a commanding place. Jesus was from God and was therefore above all earthly commandments and understandings. It was his way and his spirit that should define the position of Christians on everything. The spirit would trump flesh at every turn!

What does this mean in terms of our lives as Christians today? It can probably best be told as another story from D.T. Niles, the Sri Lankan evangelist I heard many years ago.

It was shortly after World War Two, said Niles, and the World Council of Churches was anxious to send some of its representatives to make contact with the Orthodox churches from whom it had become separated during the war. Three men were dispatched to Greece. One was Dr. Robert Mackie, moderator of the Church of Scotland. The other two were nameless Plymouth Brethren ministers. The local clerics, so long cut off from the outside world, were overjoyed to see the fellow clergymen.

One priest was so ecstatic that he couldn't do enough to

7. Ernst Käsemann, *Jesus Means Freedom* (SCM, 1969).

make them welcome. First he brought out what was left of a box of Havana cigars a parishioner had given him before the war. Dr. Mackie took one, bit the end off, lit it, puffed on it, and said what a fine cigar it was.

"No, thank you," the Plymouth Brethren said somewhat icily, "we don't smoke!"

Fearing that he had made a *faux pas* with the two clergy, the priest was eager to make amends. So he went down into the cave under his house and returned with a flagon of his best wine. Dr. Mackie accepted a glass, sniffed its bouquet, rolled a bit of it around on his tongue, then took a good swallow and said what a wonderful wine it was. Again, the Plymouth Brethren distinguished themselves by drawing themselves up and announcing that they did not drink.

Afterward, as the three visitors were back in their Jeep and headed up the rocky little road out of the village, the two Plymouth Brethren turned on Dr. Mackie with a vengeance. "Dr. Mackie," they said, "do you mean to tell us that you are the moderator of the Church of Scotland and a representative of the World Council of Churches and you both smoke and drink?!"

Poor Dr. Mackie had had about all of his companions that he could endure.

"No, dammit, I don't!" he replied. "But somebody had to be a Christian!"

Mackie was right.

And Niles was right in telling the story.

And we'll be right whenever the occasion demands such an answer and we give it.

For Jesus was above the law, and he always placed love before it.

And this is why Mark set this story at the beginning of Jesus' ministry, as a signal to remind us that this is the major insight of the whole Christian faith, and that dogma and moralism will always come in poor seconds to love and acceptance.

Where the Seed Falls

Mark 4:1-9

By any estimate, this is a remarkable parable. It has been called the Parable of the Sower, the Parable of the Seed, and the Parable of the Soils, and there is good reason for each emphasis. For centuries preachers and evangelists have appealed to it to explain and comfort themselves for a small ratio of converts to the amount of effort they have expended declaring the gospel. It is not their fault if much of the ground on which their seed falls is stony and impassive. William Carey, a self-taught linguist who in 1772 went as the first appointee of the newly formed British Missionary Society to India, labored for years without winning a single soul to Christ. We can only suppose that he read and reread this story of Jesus, consoling himself that he was faithfully casting his seed but that it simply would not grow in that thin, inhospitable soil.

But when we study the parable not as an entity in itself, which has been our custom, but as the introduction to a group of stories that in *Hidden Mark* I have called the Touchstone Passage of the Gospel, it assumes even more significance. For in the two chapters of material following this story in the Gospel, we are given a magnificent insight into exactly what the seed is that falls on different kinds of soils. There are three brief parables of Jesus about the nature of the kingdom, each relating to the physical, inanimate world. Then there is the awe-inspiring story of Jesus' calming the sea when a storm was threatening to capsize the boat filled with disciples, which I have argued is actually a post-resurrection story demonstrating how Jesus enables the beleaguered early church to survive under threatening conditions. And that is followed by three stories in which Jesus transforms the lives of three needy persons, the Gadarene demoniac, the woman with an issue of blood, and the daughter of the synagogue leader, who has actually died and is raised by Jesus.

The first three stories are about inanimate objects and the last three are about human beings. And both—the inanimate world and the world of human beings—are radically transformed by the Christ whose power over the rampaging sea is a dramatic picture of his resurrection!

This, the transforming power of Christ, is the seed every witness is to sow.

And what a seed it is! What enormous changes it can effect in any landscape where it is sown and given a chance to spring up!

But part of the burden of the parable is to remind us that, regardless of how wonderful the seed is, it doesn't always find good soil, take root, and spring up with verdant new life. In fact, this section of Mark's Gospel doesn't end with the stories of the inanimate objects and the human beings who are dramatically affected by Christ's presence. It ends with the story that follows all of these, the one in which Jesus returns to his home synagogue, in Capernaum, and astounds the crowd by his teaching. But when he has finished speaking, the old men in the crowd begin to pick him apart.

"Isn't this the carpenter," they ask, "the son of Mary and the brother of James and Joses and Judas and Simon? And don't his sisters live here with us? How could he possibly be important?!"

And then we receive this tragic statement: "*He could do no deed of power there, except that he laid his hands on a few sick people and cured them. And he was amazed at their unbelief.*"*

Do you see how this is the natural conclusion to a body of material that began with a parable about the different kinds of soil into which a sower's seed falls? Mark has Jesus tell the parable; then Mark gives us this splendid array of transformation stories, with the story of the resurrected Christ at their center; and finally he tells this sad story about how Jesus was rejected by the people in Capernaum who knew him and could not get beyond their knowing him to accepting that he might be the Savior sent from God.

Clearly, Mark wanted us—his readers—to see that the failure of the gospel to be effective when it is preached owes more to the hardness of the soil than anything else. One would have thought the people in the synagogue in Capernaum would have gone all out for Jesus, that they would have shouted and lifted him on their shoulders and carried him through the city, calling out, "Come, everybody, and see the Savior of the world!" But their hearts weren't open to him. They thought they knew everything about him but they didn't know anything. The Lord of the universe was in their midst and all they could do was say, "We know his mother and brothers and sisters, so he couldn't possibly be the Christ."

In light of this whole passage, we know a lot about Jesus'

---

* Mark 6:5-6, my italics.

concept of evangelism. He had experienced enough rejection from people who should have known better to have a very realistic picture of it. "Don't sweat it," he was saying. "Cast your seed. If it grows, great. If it doesn't, you're not responsible."

It's as simple as that.

Unfortunately, a lot of us haven't heard him on the subject. We live with numerical anxiety, worried that if we don't convert and baptize enough people we've failed to do our duty. We plan every marketing strategy imaginable—ads on TV, banners across the street, pack-the-pew night, emotional appeals for conversion, every kind of Madison Avenue trick we can pull to get people to come to church, join the church, and support the church. We become as caught up in the culture as toothpaste hucksters and used-car salesmen.

With Jesus, it was clear and simple. Cast the seed. Tell people about the one who calms the sea and saves us in the storms of life. If they don't listen, if they aren't buying—well, they didn't listen to Jesus himself, so why would they listen to us? Later, he would tell the disciples that if they took the news of God's kingdom to a village and the people there didn't listen, they shouldn't be upset. They should just shake the dust off their feet and move on (Luke 9:3).

That's what real evangelism is. It isn't all the razzle-dazzle presentations with big choirs and melt-your-heart soloists. It isn't crowds and long invitation hymns. It's telling people about the Master of wind and sea and then letting them make what they will of it. If they're receptive and thoughtful, the seed may spring up to produce an abundant transformation in their lives. If they aren't—well, they're like the hard, rocky soil where nothing will grow. Don't lose sleep over it.

I don't know many ministers who are this relaxed about preaching the gospel, do you? In fact, I tried to think of one who is, and the only one I could think of isn't actually real. He's the character named Father Mulcahy in the old *M*A*S*H* TV series. Do you remember him? A blondish man, wore glasses, had a kind of cherubic smile. He also had a slightly high-pitched voice that sometimes bobbled and failed him when he got in a tight situation or was tense about giving a homily. He was a Roman Catholic chaplain in an army field hospital somewhere in Korea, and most of the people around him were Protestants or out-and-out secularists, not fellow Catholics. But he had a good spirit. He did what he could and let it go at that. He was always faithful to his duties and invariably loving and generous to everybody. It didn't matter to him that he wasn't the hottest priest anybody ever met and couldn't convert his closest friends to religion. He seemed to have an unshakable confidence that God would take care of everything.

Maybe it's a gnostic thing. The important thing is to bring people into the secret, let them know that Jesus is with us, taking care of the things we can't manage. What they do with the knowledge is their responsibility, not ours. So we can stop measuring ourselves by Billy Graham and Joel Osteen and all the other big evangelicals. We can trust in God and be thankful for the people who do turn out to be like rich topsoil, so that the gospel flourishes in their lives.

People like Carl, who was a highly respected lighting director at CBS in Hollywood. My friend Jack Hayford, the gracious pastor of the Church in the Way, on the outskirts of Los Angeles, went to see Carl in the hospital, where he had only a few hours to live. Carl was a man of deep faith. When he saw Jack enter his room, he said, "Pastor Jack, you know when you're in my business it's the combination of lights, the skill at blending things together in order to create special effects—that's what the job's about."

Jack nodded. He understood.

"Well," said Carl, "this morning I woke up, and in the quiet of my heart Jesus spoke to me, and he said, 'Carl, how would you like to direct a sunset?'"

Think about that a moment. Let that beautiful picture sink in.

Then give thanks for Jesus—for the one who calms the sea and makes everything all right for those who have been good soil, those in whom the news of the kingdom has taken root and grown to fullness.

What more do we need in this life?

The Master of Wind and Sea
—An Easter Sermon

Mark 4:35-41

Easter—all those great biblical stories—Mary Magdalene, seeing Jesus and thinking he was the gardener—Jesus walking with the disciples on the road to Emmaus and their recognizing him when he broke the bread at table—the other disciples in the Upper Room with the doors bolted, and suddenly Jesus was there with them as if by magic—that appearance at the Sea of Galilee, when the disciples were fishing and catching nothing and Jesus called to them from the shore and told them to let down their nets on the other side.

How many sermons from how many pulpits in how many lands across how many years!

But there is another story that gets overlooked because we have failed to realize it is an Easter story too. It's the one in our text this morning, from the fourth chapter of Mark. We sometimes fail to recognize it as an Easter text because it isn't at the end of the Gospel where we expect to find such stories. The location tricks us. It makes us think it was an ordinary miracle story, not an Easter story. It looks like a simple miracle story.

But it isn't. It's an *Easter* story!

To understand this, we have to look at the surrounding bits of the Gospel. First, there were those three brief parables of

Jesus about the nature of the heavenly kingdom. Jesus says the kingdom is like a farmer who lights a lamp and sets it on a stand, where it dispels the darkness. Then he says the kingdom is like a barren field where a farmer scattered some seed. He went to bed and got up and went to bed and got up—a quaint way of saying the days passed—and one morning he got up and saw that the whole field had sprung up with new life. And finally Jesus says the kingdom of God is like a tiny mustard seed—you've seen one, in those little Lucite baubles they sell in the Holy Land for necklaces and bracelets—and when it grows up it turns into an enormous bush where all the birds of the air make their nests.

Then comes the story of Jesus' calming the sea during a terrible storm. We'll come back to that.

After that, there are three more stories, this time about human beings. First is the one about that violent lunatic who attacked everybody who came near him, and how Jesus cast his demons into a herd of swine that ran headlong into the sea, leaving the man as serene and peaceful as a civil servant at tea time. The second is about a woman "with an issue of blood"—a menstrual flow that hasn't ceased for years—who reached out in the crowd and touched the hem of Jesus' robe and was instantly healed. And the third story is about a young girl, the daughter of the local synagogue president, who died, and Jesus took her hand and ordered her to return from death, rejoicing her parents and all the others who had been mourning their loss.

Seven stories in all, with the one about Jesus and the storm in the very middle. That's the Easter story.

We've long mistaken it for something else—for an ordinary

tale about a miracle. Jesus was asleep in the boat. The disciples were rowing. A sudden storm arose. The Sea of Galilee, because it is shallow and the banks on its sides are in many places very steep, has always been prone to sudden, tumultuous storms.

"Master!" the disciples shouted. "Wake up! Do something! Don't you care if we perish?!"

And Jesus awakened, arose, and quelled the storm. Mark says the sea became "dead calm."

Like the three parables of the kingdom that precede it and the three stories about human beings that follow it, it is a story of dramatic transformation. That's amazing, when you think about it. Seven stories, and every one of them about an incredible change or transformation—a dark room turned to light, a barren field abloom with crops, a tiny seed that became a giant bush, a tempest-driven sea made calm, a crazy man restored to his senses, a sick woman healed, and a dead girl brought back to life.

And the middle story—the one about Jesus and the sea— is the one responsible for the change in all the others. That's because it is no ordinary story at all. It is an Easter story, what scholars call a "post-resurrection" story, embedded here in an early part of Mark's Gospel instead of being set at the end like the stories in the other Gospels. Think of these seven stories as a series of seven paintings, if you will, each featuring a remarkable transformation. And the painting of Jesus calming the sea stands taller than all the others, for it is the one that effects the transformation in all the others.

Think about it a moment, for it is a startling new way of understanding the story.

Then, if you're still not convinced that it is an Easter story and not merely a miracle narrative, let me point you to one very interesting detail. Jesus was asleep in the boat. That's part of the story, a vital part. Because, a little later, in the story of the girl Jesus raised from the dead, when Jesus arrived at her father's house the mourners outside told him there was no point in going inside because she was already dead.

"The child is not dead," said Jesus, "but sleeping."[1]

What a remarkable thing to say! Of course the girl was dead. They knew dead when they saw it. The life had left her. Her heart was no longer beating. She was already cold in death.

But Mark told the story this way because he wanted us to see the connection. Jesus was asleep in the boat. He too was dead. The disciples were being severely threatened by a storm. The boat was the early church. In Christian iconography, the boat was often a symbol of the church, because many of the first Christians were fishermen and because they often worshiped at sea to avoid persecution. Jesus rose from the dead when the church was threatened by persecution and made the sea calm again. He saved the early church by his resurrection from death!

Take another minute to think about it. It's a big story. A huge story. We aren't used to thinking this way. Mark tricked us by putting the story where he did.

But now see what the Gospel is saying. It's proclaiming the vast difference the resurrection of Jesus makes in everything. *Everything!* The dark room that becomes flooded with light. The field that was barren and is now abloom. The tiny seed that grows into an enormous bush. And people too—the man who became sane and peaceful after his demons left him, the woman whose menstrual flow was healed, the little girl who

1. Mark 5:39.

was raised from the dead. Inanimate nature and animate nature. Things and people. All of them changed, dramatically transformed, by the risen Christ!

Not an Easter story? It may well be the greatest Easter story of all!

What does it mean to us today? How does it affect us—our lives, our loved ones, our work, our plans, our daily existence, our fate when we die? Don't you see, it means that everything about our lives is different because Christ has been raised from death.

It's what St. Paul exclaimed in his letter to the Corinthians, "O death, where is thy sting? O grave, where is thy victory? Death has been swallowed up in victory!"[2]

We are the people of the victory! No matter what our life stories have been or what they are now—some of us are sick, some are in wheel chairs, some have lost jobs, some have lost parents or spouses or children—everything is changed. It's like that little thing we do on the computer sometimes, when we highlight everything and completely transform the entire text we've been writing. *Click, click, click,* and it's totally different!

Let me give you one illustration of it. It's about a dear friend of mine named Tom.

Tom was a minister. One night when he and his wife had gone out to celebrate an anniversary, their eight-year-old son accidentally shot and killed his older brother. When they came home, they found their house surrounded by police cars with flashing lights, and only learned about the tragedy when they stepped inside. After that, Tom spent two years fighting a prison term for having had an unregistered firearm in his home, even though it was a family relic that wasn't supposed to be in

2. 1 Corinthians 15:54-55, order reversed.

working order. When the court finally sentenced him to ten years on parole, he and his wife and son moved to another state, and he became the minister of a different church.

Meanwhile, Tom's car had been rear-ended by another vehicle, severely jostling his brain. He soon showed signs of Parkinson's disease. Within a few years, his speech became so difficult to understand that he had to retire from the ministry. He was only 52 years old and could not find other employment.

His son, who had become a fine young actor, dancer, and singer, got a part in a Broadway musical, then got busted for drug usage and committed to a fifty-day rehabilitation program in another state. Tom and his wife decided to get a divorce. His mother died and his father had lung cancer. He moved in with his father because his father was afraid to be alone at night.

Tom's severance pay from his church ran out before his disability payments from the government began to arrive.

On top of everything, he wrote me in an e-mail, his dog was hit by a car and died.

But in spite of everything—this catalog of horrors—Tom wrote this e-mail to his son in the rehabilitation camp:

> I had a bad night last night. I woke up at 3 a.m. and couldn't turn over. I went through the alphabet, thinking of Bible verses beginning with A, B, C, and so on. Then I did the same with the first words of hymns. Everything seemed so hopeless and my spirit was so low. Then I began to notice that the darkness was not empty. There was a sense of presence, and it was friendly. It was the infinite, awesome Creator God. Then there was Christ's gentle command, "Take my hand." I did, and then the

once silent music audibly filled all the space around
me and the Spirit moved ever so slowly to the
music, drawing my whole being into the dance of
the dark. And I was comforted and not alone.

Tom's story is one of the most beautiful witnesses I have
ever known to the dramatic power of the risen Christ in a person's life. Here was a man so obviously broken and defeated by
life, by fate or whatever you want to call it, and yet he was so
obviously triumphant in Christ. He listened to the silent music
and heard Christ calling him to dance, so he danced. In his
heart and mind, this man with Parkinson's disease, so crushed
by life's harsh circumstances, danced with the risen Lord!

That is an Easter story. And it is precisely what the Easter
story in Mark's Gospel is all about. It's about the dramatic
transformation Christ's resurrection has made in our lives. We
are all being threatened by a great storm on the sea of life—
lightning flashing on every side, thunder rumbling through the
sky, and the waves rising around us like great liquid horses
bucking and stampeding—and the sleeping Jesus awakes form
his sleep, stands in the prow of the ship, and says, "Peace, be
still!"

It isn't any wonder the disciples all wondered at him, and
declared him "the Master of wind and sea." It isn't an overstate-
ment to say that his resurrection was the defining moment in
the history of the world. And, most important of all to each of
us, it is—right now and in this place—the defining fact of our
lives.

The Mother Who Changed
the History of the World

Mark 7:24-30; 6:30-44; 8:1-10

Have you ever gone on vacation hoping to get away from everything and you hadn't any more than got into your hotel when the phone rang and it was somebody wanting you to do something? I did. In fact, my wife and I had flown to London, England, and had just settled down in our hotel room for the night when the phone rang and I heard the voice of a rather strident woman from my parish back in America who said she too was in London. She had called to tell me about an experience she had earlier in the evening when she got stuck in a somewhat narrow bathtub of her room. When the water drained out of the tub, she had been suctioned to the bottom. Her daughter, unable to get her out, covered her with a sheet and called a bellhop. The ingenious bellhop simply ran more water in the tub, which allowed the woman to extricate herself with no trouble.

I can appreciate how Jesus felt in our text when this woman—not a Jew but someone from Syria—intruded on his privacy to ask a favor. He had been dealing with wall-to-wall people in Galilee and needed a rest, so he and his disciples had traveled to the seacoast where no one would know him. But somehow this woman found out that he was a miracle healer and she had a sick daughter and she barged in on him to ask a favor.

I can imagine it, can't you?

The disciples were tired too, and were doubtless glad to get away from the throngs of people in Galilee. Peter, James, and John were out walking along the seashore, probably curious to see what kind of boats and gear the local fishermen used when they went out on the Mediterranean. Philip, Andrew, and Bartholomew strolled down to the village market, where they fell to talking with the old men who sat under the plane trees. Naturally, they talked about their Master, Jesus, and what an important figure he was back home. It wasn't long before the whole town was talking about the miracle worker who was staying in a house down by the wharf.

The woman in the story, a nameless Greek woman from the region known as Syrophoenicia, was probably shopping in the market when she heard about Jesus. The minute she heard about the miracles he had done, her heart beat faster and she knew she had to solicit his help for her little daughter, who lay sick in bed with a high fever. She lost no time in finding the house where he was staying. Maybe Matthew was sitting there on the doorstep whittling when she approached and asked if he was the miracle worker. No, said Matthew; she was seeking his Master, who was asleep in the house.

"Then wake him up!" I can imagine the woman's saying. "I have something for him to do!"

Her daughter was extremely sick, she told Jesus. She needed a miracle.

Jesus was reluctant.

"Let the children be fed first," he said, "for it is not fair to take the children's food and throw it to the dogs."[1]

Sounds rude, doesn't it? We don't expect Jesus, of all people, to behave so brusquely with a woman in need. It doesn't sound like him. But we have to remember that Mark has a purpose in this. It isn't just a good story, it's a yarn with real significance.

"Sir," responds the woman, "even the dogs under the table eat the children's crumbs."[2]

Now we miss something here by not knowing the original Greek that Mark was writing in, for the word she used for "dogs" was *kunariois*, which meant "little dogs"—the kind of dogs that were kept inside, not the big, mangy looking dogs that roamed the streets and countryside. Even the little dogs under the table, she argued, are allowed to eat the crumbs dropped by the children.

Maybe Jesus liked her spunk. Or maybe Mark was making his point. Either way, it was a remarkable scene for those times, because women had no status at all in the world of males. It was cheeky of her to invade Jesus' privacy in the first place; and it was doubly cheeky of her to argue with him when he said he wouldn't help her. But this is an argument in favor of Mark's being a Gnostic document, because the Gnostics held women in much higher esteem than most people of that day. They had women priests in the mystery religions of the area, and Gnostic Christians, like their counterparts in other religions, treated women as the equals of men.

At any rate, Jesus gave in to her argument. "For saying that," he said, "you may go—the demon has left your daughter."[3]

She went home and found that it was true. Her daughter was all right again.

It's a sweet little story, granted. But it doesn't seem to justify

1. Mark 7:27.
2. Mark 7:28.
3. Mark 7:29.

the extravagance of the sermon title, does it? "The Mother Who Changed the History of the World."

Wait, though. There's more.

We have to see the story, as we do most of Mark's stories, in the context of the Gospel as a whole, so that we understand what Mark was getting at.

If we turn back to Mark 6:30-44, we find the famous story of Jesus' feeding of an immense crowd in the wilderness—5,000 people in all!—with only a few loaves of bread and two fish. It is a fabulous, mind-boggling story, really, all that food for so many people, and twelve baskets full of food left over when they had eaten. But it was a very important story to the early Christians, for they doubtless saw references in it to the Lord's Supper, and how Jesus was always bringing refreshment and sustenance to his people in wilderness places, just as he rescued the disciples from the storm at sea.

Then if we turn the other way, to Mark 8:1-10, there is another story of a feeding miracle. In this story, Jesus feeds 4,000 people in a wilderness setting, and once again there is much food left over—seven basketsful, in fact.

But there is another significant difference, aside from the size of the crowds and the amount of food left over from each feeding. In the second feeding, according to Mark 7:31, Jesus is in the area known as the Decapolis. This area lay southeast of Galilee, adjacent to the area of Samaria, and was settled mainly by non-Jews. The first feeding had taken place in Galilee—*Jewish* territory. The second was in the Decapolis—*Gentile* territory.

The difference in locations is emphasized by the numbers associated with the two stories. In the first story, of a feeding in Jewish territory, there were 5,000 people. Five thousand is a multiple of five, the sacred number of the Jewish Torah. And there were twelve baskets full of food remaining—for the number of the tribes of Israel. In the second story, the one about a feeding in Gentile territory, there were 4,000 people—a multiple of the four corners of the earth. And there were seven baskets full of food remaining—the base number in the number seventy, for the seventy nations of the world, which people in that time thought there were.

Jesus had moved, in other words, from a ministry to the Jews to a ministry among the Gentiles. And the springboard from one to the other was his encounter with the Gentile mother in the region of Tyre and Sidon, where he was trying to vacation. In Mark's view, at least, it was Jesus' meeting with this mother who had an ill daughter that led Jesus to broaden the scope of his activities and include the Gentiles in his work of teaching and healing!

So you can see that she literally altered the history of the world. If she had not interrupted Jesus' rest by the seashore and insisted that he perform a miracle for her daughter, it is possible that he would never have expanded his ministry beyond the Jewish people he had originally planned to go to. And, if he hadn't expanded his ministry, the chronicles of early Christianity, and therefore of the whole world, would have been significantly different.

I mentioned the part that Gnosticism might have played in this important shift. And Mark's Gospel, as the first of all the extant accounts of Jesus' life and ministry, doubtless set a tone for the regard of women that was followed by the other Gospels. In no other documents of the time were women so highly regarded and honorably treated.

Think of the sensitivity accorded women in the four Gospels. First, there was the reverence accorded to Mary, the mother of Jesus, and her role in the birth and rearing of our Lord. Clearly, there were several women who traveled with Jesus and the disciples, some of them helping to pay the expenses of the little group. There were the wonderful stories of the woman at the well, Mary and Martha, the poor widow who gave her entire living to the temple treasury, and the women who went to Jesus' tomb on the first Easter Sunday. And, taking his clue from the Gospel writers, Paul frequently alludes very positively to various women in the churches of the several cities to which he addressed his epistles. The women of the New Testament were loving, guiding, nurturing forces in the shaping of our religious understanding, and we owe them an inestimable debt.

All of this was made even clearer with the recovery of the so-called Nag Hammadi Library, those ancient Gnostic manuscripts recovered near the Nile River in 1945. In the brief but important little *Gospel of Mary*, Jesus' disciples are described as fearful and irresolute after the Savior's departure. "How shall we go to the gentiles and preach the gospel of the kingdom of the Son of Man?" they complained. "If they did not spare him, how will they spare us?" But Mary—actually Mary Magdalene—stood and addressed them. "Do not weep and do not grieve nor be irresolute," she bade them, "for his grace will be entirely with you and will protect you."[4] Apparently her little speech made a great difference in their attitudes.

Then Simon Peter approached her and said, "Sister, we know that the Savior loved you more than the rest of women.

4. *The Nag Hammadi Library in English*, ed. James M. Robinson (Harper & Row, 1988), p. 525.

Tell us the words of the Savior which you remember—which you know (but) we do not, nor have we heard them."[5] And Mary commenced to narrate for them a vision in which she had spoken with Christ about the nature of the soul, the spirit, and the mind—a philosophical disquisition that would have been dear to the hearts of Gnostic Christians.

The woman in our text—the mother of the little girl with a demon—was one of the beautiful women of the New Testament. She was beautiful in her love for her daughter. She was a real mother. We are given the feeling that she might have crawled over splintered glass for the sake of her little girl. And her love—her natural human love, her motherly love—became the pivot on which the entire ministry of Jesus turned!

A mother's love is like that.

I remember a similar mother I met at a spiritual retreat in Kentucky. Her name was Margaret Howard. About sixty-five at the time, Margaret was a good, solid woman of the hills who managed a small bookstore in Richmond, Kentucky called the Miracle Book Room. I was to learn why she called it that.

Margaret had an eighth-grade education. She married when she was only fourteen, and had to leave school. But she was a woman of rare qualities. When one of her daughters had a brain tumor at the age of seven, surgeons removed most of the right hemisphere of her brain. They told Margaret she would be a mere vegetable for the rest of her life. Margaret wouldn't accept their judgment. She nursed the girl and cared for her as only a mother would.

One day she saw a newspaper article about a special operation being performed in Canada that might improve her daughter's condition. Pursuing the information, she learned

5. Ibid.

that the surgery would cost $7,000, which was more than Margaret earned in a year. But that didn't stop her. She prayed for God's help in raising the money for the operation. A reporter put a story in the local newspaper about her ambition for her daughter, and more than $10,000 poured into the newspaper office to send Margaret and her daughter to Canada.

Margaret had never made such a journey before, and didn't realize she would need passports for her and her daughter. When they arrived in Canada, the airlines would not permit them to deplane without passports. Unwilling to be turned away at this stage, Margaret demanded to see an airport official, and asked for a telephone connection with top government officials in Canada. She told the person she talked with that she had brought her daughter all the way from Kentucky to have an operation that would enrich her life. Because she mentioned the governor of Kentucky several times, the person she talked with got the idea that she was related to him, and eventually agreed to send an ambulance to take her and her daughter to the hospital.

Later someone asked her, "Are you from the governor?" "No," she said. "Are you a friend of his?" she was asked. "I didn't even vote for him," Margaret said.

The doctors at the hospital took X-rays, studied them, and said they did not want to operate. Margaret said to them, "There's a power higher than you that obviously wants you to."

Bowing to this juggernaut of a woman, the doctors operated, and the surgery was successful. The girl lived an almost normal life for several years and died of natural causes while still a young woman.

Today I almost never read the story of the Gentile mother

in this text in Mark without thinking of Margaret Howard. God invented something pretty special when he invented mothers. They put an awful lot of love and care into the world. In fact, they are a never-ending supply.

And Jesus responded to the love and care of that Syrophoenician woman. It was as if she reminded him of God's love and care for all his children, the Gentiles as well as the Jews, and he turned to his ministry to the world because of her love for her child.

Her love was the hinge on which all history turned!

And isn't it interesting, we don't even know her name. Such an important woman, and the disciples neglected to learn who she was or to remember her name after the event. We know she was Greek. Perhaps her name was Helen or Dora or Theodora. Theodora means "gift of God." That would have been an appropriate name for her. It's a shame we don't know, because if we did there would be churches erected in her memory all over the world. The Church of St. Helen or the Cathedral of St. Theodora.

But perhaps there is significance in the fact that she remained nameless, that this wonderful mother has gone down in history as our great unknown benefactress; for aren't most of the wonderful deeds of mothers done in silence and anonymity, without the world's knowing who did them? That is part of what being a mother is about—loving without credit, pouring oneself into others for the pure joy of doing it.

How many mothers, like this faithful, ardent mother in our scripture, have really changed the history of the world and we never acknowledged it? How many are changing the world today, quietly, softly instilling love and human values in their children, praying for their children, making their children whole in a fragmented society and thereby helping to make society itself whole?

Thank God for mothers! They should all be called Theodora, for they are all gifts from God.

The Savior Who Appears
in the Dark of the Night

Mark 6:45-52

Another emergency in a storm at sea—you'd think the disciples would have learned to stay off the water at night, wouldn't you?—only this time Jesus was not with them. He was up on a nearby mountain where he had gone to pray. And yet at the height of the storm, when they thought all was lost, he was aware of their danger and came striding toward them like a ghost gliding through the waves and spray.

What do you make of such a story? Was it only a tall tale concocted by the disciples to glorify their Master? Or did it actually happen just as Mark described it? What was Mark's purpose in telling the story and putting it exactly where he placed it in the unfolding of his Gospel?

Once more, after encountering the artful placement of the earlier story about a storm at sea so that it informed three earlier stories and three later ones with its powerful significance, we are encouraged to look around and see if Mark had any such design in locating this storm narrative where he did. Almost at once we see the possibility that he did.

In Mark 6:30-44, he told the story of the feeding of the 5,000 Jewish followers—mass communion in the wilderness.

Then, in Mark 7:24-30, he narrated the tale of the Syrophoenician woman who besought him to cast a demon out of her
daughter, which we have already observed becomes the bridge
between Jesus' mission to the Jews and his subsequent mission
to the Gentiles. In Mark 8:1-10, he proceeded to the story of
the feeding of the 4,000 Gentile followers in the Decapolis area.
And, just as the calming-of-the-sea story in Mark 4:35-41 was
the keystone passage of the earlier group of narratives, this
calming-of-the-sea story is the keystone for the two feeding
stories, shedding its light backward on one and forward on the
other.

So what does it say and how is it related to the other stories?

If we allow our imaginations a little freedom, we might see
a relationship between Jesus' being up on a mountain praying
and the iconography of the early church that sometimes pic-
tured either God or Jesus or the two of them together on a
mountain *as if they were in heaven.*

It isn't much of a stretch for the imagination, is it? After all,
the Greeks had long had a tradition of picturing their gods—
Zeus and Hera and Poseidon and all the others—as residing
on Mount Olympus. When the Romans adopted the Greek
pantheon as their own—or, more accurately, absorbed it during
the centuries when Greece ruled most of the Mediterranean
lands—they continued to depict the gods as dwelling on a
mountain. Some evidence suggests that they replaced Mount
Olympus with Mount Aetna, but other evidence indicates that
they merely changed the names of the gods but not the name
of their lofty abode.

In the first calming-of-the-sea story, Jesus was supposedly

"asleep" in the boat, although, as we have seen in comparing Jesus' own statement about the daughter of the synagogue leader, that she was only "sleeping" when she was actually dead, it was a way of saying that Jesus was dead but rose from the dead to rescue his followers when they were in peril.

In this, the second calming-of-the-sea story, Jesus is actually in heaven communing with God, not merely praying on a mountain, when he becomes aware of the storm that is threatening the well-being of his followers.

It is no wonder, then, that when the disciples behold him coming near their boat in the early hours of the morning, they think he is a ghost. He is, actually, in at least one sense. He is the transcendent or supernatural Christ who is appearing to them in a time of desperate need.

Notice what Jesus says to his followers when they cry out in terror: "Take heart, it is I; do not be afraid."[1]

That sounds simple enough, doesn't it? And so it has been generally interpreted through the centuries, as a mere word of comfort and assurance that it is actually their Lord and not an ordinary ghost.

But let's look at it again, unpacking it as we do so.

First, Jesus says "Take heart." Does that sound at all familiar? It should. One of the oldest phrases in early Christian worship, one that has found its way into numerous musical settings in the years since then, is the Latin *Sursum corda*, or "Lift up your hearts!", to which the traditional response is "We lift them up to the Lord!" These are phrases generally associated with Easter and the resurrection. In Orthodox churches they are still frequently spoken as a friendly greeting from one Christian to another on Easter morning.

1. Mark 6:49.

Next, let's consider the apparently simple little statement "It is I." That's straightforward and uncomplicated, isn't it? The sort of thing a parent might utter to a child in a darkened room, "It's me."

But this too has a history that expands its significance.

In the Septuagint, the Greek version of the Old Testament, the words with which God answers Moses in Exodus 3:14, when Moses asks God's name so he can use it before Pharaoh and God answers tersely, "I AM WHO I AM," are, in the Greek, *ego eimi*—the same words used by Jesus in the Greek text of Mark 6:49! What are we to conclude? That this usage is merely coincidental? Surely, when coupled with the words "Take heart," it begs to be identified with God's response to Moses, doesn't it?

To the disciples, cowering in a boat being shaken by a fierce tempest in the dark of the night, it must have seemed as if the ghostly figure who came to their rescue was identifying himself with the great I AM! There was good reason for them not to be afraid—they were about to be rescued by God's incarnate presence himself.

In this story, there is no peremptory command to the wind and waves to be still. Instead, Jesus merely gets into the boat with them, and when he does the wind immediately dies. His presence is enough to insure calmness and safety. Nothing can touch them when he is in their midst.

The passage merely concludes: "And they were utterly astounded, for they did not understand about the loaves, but their hearts were hardened."[2]

I said "merely," but again there is much to unpack in Mark's brief report. He says they were astounded because they didn't

2. Mark 6:52.

understand "about the loaves"—about his feeding of the 5,000, which Jesus had accomplished with the five loaves and two fishes they had turned up for him to bless.

What didn't they understand? That he was the Christ, the Messiah, the Son of Man, the transcendent One who represented God Almighty himself, and for whom no miracle of any kind was too great. He would throw it up to them later, in Mark 8:14-21, when he would accuse them of having their hearts hardened and not being able to see or hear what had transpired in their very presence.

Again, a little understanding of Gnosticism is helpful in interpreting the text. To the Gnostic Christians, every one was blind to the transcendent dimension of things until God opened their eyes and enabled them to see the miraculous all around them. This is why the passage in Mark 8:14-21, when Jesus accuses the disciples of being blind and deaf, is followed immediately by a symbolic passage in Mark 8:22-26 in which Jesus makes a blind man see. And why, in Mark 10:46-52, it is a blind man sitting beside the road who recognizes that Jesus is the Messiah and calls out to him, while most of the others present, including the disciples, cannot see what he sees.

Now, what are we to make of this text in our own lives today? What does it say to us about Jesus, about the storms in our lives, and about the nature of Christian faith?

I had a conversation with my friend Donna the other day. Donna is a member of the church I pastored in Los Angeles several years ago. At that time she worked for one of the big film studios. I knew she had been battling cancer for several years. She recently began a new kind of chemotherapy that her doctor is giving her as a sort of last chance medication. She had nine infusions of the chemo in twelve weeks, then a respite, and was beginning another nine infusions. After the second one this time, she began running a high fever and was very sick for several days. She phoned me from a rehabilitation center where she was recovering and told me that, as she put it, she had "almost bought the farm." But then she went on to say how peaceful she had been through the whole ordeal because she felt the presence of Christ with her at all times.

"I was ready to go," she said, "because I know I can trust him with my soul."

Isn't that exactly what our text is about? People caught in almost impossible situations in the middle of the night, with the waves threatening to take them under forever. Women like Donna, with cancer. Men battling prostate cancer or heart trouble. Fathers and mothers dealing with sickly or rebellious children. Children feeling all alone when beset by personal failure or bullying or rejection by their peers. People out of work and unable to find jobs. Others losing their homes because they can't meet their mortgage payments. The list goes on and on. There are almost no limits to the sufferings of people everywhere. We are born to suffering, Job said, "as the sparks fly upward."

We are like the disciples out on the lake in that boat, with the waves rising above them on every side, ready to suck them under and send them down to their watery deaths. And then the transcendent Savior comes walking through the storm as if he were a ghost, completely unthreatened by the storms that are destroying our lives.

"Take heart," he says, "it is I. Do not be afraid."

It is I. I AM WHO I AM.

Relax. Don't be afraid any more. We are safe with him. Nothing can really touch us when our hearts are given to him, when we know him and trust him.

In the early church, among the beleaguered Christians of that day, it meant not even fearing to be cast into the arena with lions and tigers. To Martin Luther, it meant not being afraid of what the powers in Rome could do to him when he stood up for what he truly believed. To thousands of Christians in every land who have withstood pogroms and persecutions for their beliefs, it has meant walking ahead with their chins held high in spite of threats of death and humiliation. To all of us struggling with our own personal demons—with family problems, sickness and disease, alcoholism and drug addiction, poverty and debt, loneliness and betrayal—it means not having to be afraid any more and not being alone any more.

All we have to do is know him as Lord and trust him to get in the boat with us. That's the sum total. Just know him and trust him.

How Stupid Can You Be?

Mark 8:14-21

We do a lot of dumb things, don't we? I remember the time I was chopping wood near a clothes line and hit the clothes line with the axe, causing it to fly back within an inch of my head. A friend named Joe borrowed a boat and motor to go fishing. When he tried to start the motor out in the middle of the lake, it fell off its mounting and sank. Without thinking, Joe grabbed it and tried to hold on to it. It pulled him under and nearly drowned him. He and I were both almost candidates for the Darwin Awards, those annual recognitions of people who have been killed in freak accidents of their own making, like the woman who tried to put out a kitchen fire by pouring a bucket of kerosene on it and the man who sawed off a tree limb he was sitting on.

A clinical psychologist named Madeleine Van Hecke has written a book called *Blind Spots: Why Smart People Do Dumb Things*.[1] She looks at our stupidity from several perspectives. Sometimes, she says, we jump to hasty conclusions. Other times we operate out of faulty prejudices. And at still other times we simply have blind spots in our normal intelligence about things. But we are all guilty of doing dumb things from time to time, and some of them are really inexcusable.

1. Prometheus Books, 2007.

I have to believe that was the case with Jesus' disciples in
this text. They certainly exhibited an embarrassing amount of
stupidity. They were rowing Jesus across the lake to get away
from the Pharisees who were annoying him. While they were
rowing, one of them realized they had forgotten to bring any
bread. There was one loaf in the boat, but that wasn't nearly
enough. Two of the primary duties of a disciple were to find
nightly shelter for their master and to provide his food at the
appropriate times. So they began to feel guilty about their over-
sight, and possibly to argue among themselves about who was
most at fault.

Jesus, still thinking about the Pharisees who had been ar-
guing with him back on the land, said to them, "Watch out—
beware of the yeast of the Pharisees and the yeast of Herod."[2]
He used "yeast" in the sense of something that ferments and
spreads, like mold. In rabbinical usage of the time it implied
something evil or pernicious.

But the disciples instantly became hung up on the word
"yeast" and thought he was reminding them that they had failed
to bring any bread. "It is because we have no bread,"[3] they whis-
pered. He had pricked their guilty consciences!

Discerning what they were discussing, and amazed at their
thickheadedness, Jesus said, "Why are you talking about having
no bread? Do you still not perceive or understand? Are your
hearts hardened? Do you have eyes, and fail to see? Do you have
ears, and fail to hear? And do you not remember? When I
broke the five loaves for the five thousand, how many basketsful
of broken pieces did you collect?"

They said, "Twelve."

"And the seven for the four thousand, how many basketsful

2. Mark 8:14.
3. Mark 8:16.

of broken pieces did you collect?"

"Seven," they said.

And he concluded, "Do you not yet understand?"[4]

The irony was that these disciples, whom he had carefully chosen to be his followers, had been with him for a long time and had recently seen him feed two enormous crowds with bread to spare, and were still worried about not having any bread. They were in the presence of the greatest bread maker of all time, the *Master* of all bread making, and they were troubled about having forgotten to bring a few loaves in the boat!

How dumb can you be? How blind and insensitive?

That's the issue here, isn't it? Even Jesus' own disciples, the twelve men who had received the greatest honor ever accorded to human beings, failed to see what a transcendent, magical figure he was.

Again, this is part of the early Christian Gnostic understanding. In ancient mystery religions, even people who attended cultic meetings and had the secrets of the religions revealed to them often failed to grasp them. They saw but didn't see. They heard but didn't hear. It was the same among the Christian Gnostics—there were eminent leaders in every community who did not really understand who Jesus was, what he meant to the human situation and how God was acting through him. They assumed they knew, but they didn't.

This is why Mark made so much of Jesus' recognition by blind men. His apostles could not see who he was even though their eyes were open and they had been with him through everything. But the ones to whom God vouchsafed true vision—like Bartimaeus in Mark 10:46-52—could see what others didn't. And this is undoubtedly why, immediately following

4. Mark 18:17-21.

this passage about the blindness of the disciples, Mark described Jesus' giving sight to a blind man in the city of Bethsaida.[5] It was the great anomaly of early Christianity: the ones
with 20/20 vision were often blind, while the blind often had
perfect spiritual vision.

I said *early* Christianity. But the same has been true all
through the ages, hasn't it? Over and over, repeatedly through
the centuries, those whose special opportunities should have
equipped them to see and understand the meaning of Jesus'
messiahship didn't grasp it at all, while others, often those in
humble status or even considered reprobates, were able to see
with total clarity. How many popes and how many pastors have
been blind leaders of the blind, committing sacrilege upon sacrilege and failing to lead their flocks to a deeper understanding
of spiritual matters?

Think about the ministers and churches you know today.
How many are truly Christian? How many have become deeply
spiritual in every way by being related to the transcendent
Christ? The bulk of them, unfortunately—probably 99 percent—are merely "institutional" Christians. They grew up in
the church or started going at some point in their lives, then
began taking Jesus and the whole business of the transcendent
life for granted. They aren't thrilled to be in the presence of
God's Messiah. Most of the time, they don't even think about
it. They have simply become acculturated to whatever is said
about Jesus and the higher life, so that they hardly notice. Like
the disciples, they worry about bread and material things because they don't even know Jesus for who he really is!

It's sad. But it's true, isn't it?

This is what Mark was trying to say, that very few people—

5. Mark 8:22-26.

even those who have been in an enviable position to know all about Jesus, as the disciples were—have the least idea who he is or what it means that God sent him into our midst. Their eyes and ears have never been opened. It's as if their very hearts were hardened or calloused beyond all sensitivity.

Talk about the dumb things that smart people do! Could anything be dumber than this? Could anything be worse than to live with an outer knowledge of Jesus and never have an inner, more personal knowledge of him? I can't imagine what it would be. Surely this represents the ultimate in stupidity.

One of the worst examples of this—one I have struggled to forget but can't—was of a woman who was vice-president of the women's association in a church where I was the pastor and who was very active in many other facets of the church's program. It happened on Thanksgiving. We had enjoyed a beautiful Thanksgiving service and were standing outside in the courtyard, reluctant to leave—it was in California—when a battered looking man came up to us wearing plastic bags on his feet. His hair was long and dirty and there was blood on his face and clothes. He had AIDS, he said, and had been turned away by his family. He had spent the night in a nearby park, and during the night someone had mugged him and taken his wallet and shoes. He asked if we had any food. We didn't, I said, but I would get him some coffee.

While I was getting the coffee, which I loaded with cream and sugar, he admired a cloisonné necklace my wife was wearing and asked if he might touch it. One thing led to another, and he confessed he had not been hugged for a long time and asked if he might have a hug. My wife gladly hugged him and kissed his cheek. While I was in the church, I called a hospice and made arrangements for him to come there. I also ordered a taxi, and paid the driver to take him.

We finally left the church and drove home, greatly sobered by this sad encounter. We had barely got inside the front door when the phone rang. It was the vice-president of the women's association and she wanted to talk to my wife. "You have embarrassed your husband and embarrassed our church," she began. She assailed my wife in every way she could think of for having hugged a man who was an obvious outcast dying of AIDS.

My wife didn't know how to respond. She could hardly believe that a woman who professed to be a follower of Christ could harbor such uncharitable feelings for one of God's dear creatures. Nor could I. As much as we liked this woman and tried to understand her reasoning, we could no longer believe she knew Christ in any personal way, for her heart had obviously not been transformed by the relationship they would have had.

For a smart lady, she had behaved like a dummy.

On the other hand, I remember a man named Bart, whom I knew in another parish. Bart, a fresh looking young man in his thirties, had Lou Gehrig's disease, and wore braces on his legs to help him walk. He worked for a local nursery and was finding it more and more difficult to perform his duties. Apparently God laid a hand on him during one of our Sunday services, and he told me afterward that he had had a religious experience and would like to be baptized and join the church. In the weeks after that, I got to know Bart and his wife through several visits. I learned that they had wanted children but had not been blessed with any.

Bart's encounter with Christ transformed his life, which had been on a downward spiral because of his worsening physical problem. His spirits lifted, he began to feel better. His doctors were amazed at his improvement. A few months later, his wife became pregnant, and they were both overjoyed to be having a child. Bart became the leader of a Boy Scout troupe and seemed to thrive on the activity.

Several years later, when I was revisiting that parish, I saw Bart again. He appeared healthy and vigorous, and was as happy as any man I'd ever known.

I had no doubt that something special had happened to Bart that Sunday when he met the Lord. It had truly changed his life. The downward spiral caused by his disease had been reversed, and he seemed to be on an upward path in every way. To me, his improvement was nothing short of miraculous. He was like the people in the Gospel of Mark who actually met the Savior and had their lives changed.

When it comes to knowing Jesus, there isn't any way of predicting who will be smart and who will be blind. Perhaps that's because faith isn't always something we can control, it is something God bestows. That way no one can brag about having received it. But whoever we are and whatever we know—even if we are ministers and have a little gaggle of letters after our names—we ought to be quite humble, because it's possible to be very stupid about Jesus and think we know him when we don't know him at all.

The Miracle Jesus Had to Do Twice

Mark 8:22-26

Ifeel a certain kinship to the fellow in this text. I was born with extremely poor eyesight. Not as poor as his in the beginning, but as poor as it was in the middle, when he saw men "like trees, walking." I was very nearsighted. Anything moving looked like a tree walking unless I got close enough to be hit by it. I can remember the afternoon when I received my first pair of glasses. I was nine years old. I put on the glasses and walked down the street. I could hardly believe the transformation! Suddenly the world was in focus, vivid and colorful, for the first time in my life. So I have a strong affinity for the man in our text, albeit at a step from where he began, in total blindness.

But it is a strange text. There is something quite unique about it. It depicts the only miracle Jesus ever had to do twice.

Every other miracle recorded in the four Gospels came off a hundred percent the first time. The water changed to wine was instantly the best wine anybody ever tasted. The lame man Jesus healed by the pool of Bethsaida got up immediately and carried his pallet through the crowd. The little girl who was dead—the daughter of the synagogue leader—arose instantly when Jesus called her. But in this one case, of the man who was blind, Jesus was required to expend a second effort. The first wasn't good enough. The man's vision was only partially restored.

What are we to make of this? Mark's Gospel is full of mystery and special lessons, isn't it? So what did he intend with this narrative about a blind man who wasn't instantly healed by Jesus?[1] Given what has preceded the text—Jesus' upbraiding of the disciples for not seeing that he was the Messiah of God with unlimited powers—we must surmise that this particular story is not as much about the blind man himself as it is about seeing. It is about the miracle of seeing—or not seeing—in all of us. It is about being touched by Jesus once, and twice, and maybe even three times, in order to see clearly what God wants us to see.

It's about us, isn't it? It's *our* story. We all have trouble seeing. Even those of us with 20/20 eyesight may still be perceptually blind.

We are blind to many things—to stars in the night—to the bark on old pine trees—to the amazing feats of little insects— to the wonder of our own skin, which is the largest organ we have. Many of us have become so habitualized to our worlds— "environmentalized" was Marshall McLuhan's term—that we don't see the world any longer. Not with any freshness. Not the way Zorba saw it, in Kazantzakis' novel.

Do you remember Zorba? I have always been in love with him, I think. What a wonderful, childlike way he had of seeing the world around him. Beholding the sea again for the hundredth or thousandth or ten-thousandth time, he would exclaim, "What is that? That miracle over there, boss, that moving

1. In *The Nag Hammadi Library*, there are excerpts of an ancient Gnostic tractate called "The Discourse on the Eighth and Ninth" that describes the process by which a spiritual guide or mystagogue leads an initiate into mystical experience. The mystagogue reminds his pupil of how he gradually learned from books and conversations. The pupil remembers "the beauty that came to me in the books." "This is what you call the beauty of the soul," says the mystagogue, "the edification that came to you in stages. May the understanding come to you, and you will teach." Op. cit., p. 323.

blue, what do they call it? Sea? Sea? And what's that wearing a flowered green apron? Earth? Who was the artist who did it? It's the first time I've seen that, boss, I swear!"[2]

His boss, the narrator, says: "Like the child, he sees everything for the first time. He is forever astonished and wonders why and wherefore. Everything seems miraculous to him, and each morning when he opens his eyes he sees trees, sea, stones and birds, and is amazed."[3]

Walking along a country road and encountering an old man leading a mule, Zorba stared at it until the old man cursed him, thinking he was putting an evil eye on the animal. The boss wanted to know what made the old man cry out at him. "I was looking at his mule, that's all," said Zorba. "Didn't it strike you, boss?"

"What?" asked the boss.

"Well," answered Zorba, "that there are such things as mules in this world!"[4]

Eyes that were fresh, open, ready to see.

Most of us are even worse about seeing spiritual things, aren't we? Like Jesus' disciples, we have eyes but we don't see. Not really. We pass shoppers in the stores without observing their dreams, their disappointments, their loneliness. We sit in church by people whose hearts are breaking and never give them a second thought. We live in a world where half the people are hungry, yet we never choke on our food. Where many are sick, yet we rarely give thanks for our health. Where countless numbers are burdened, enslaved, confused, yet we seldom pray for them.

It's true, isn't it? We need to be touched again by Jesus, and made to see with fresh vision. The promise of our text, which

2. Nikos Kazantsakis, *Zorba the Greek* (Touchstone Books, 1952), p. 228.
3. Ibid., p. 151.
4. Ibid., pp. 151-152.

isn't negative after all but positive, is that he will touch us again. Not once, but again and again if necessary. Christ wants his followers to see, and he touches us in many ways.

He touches us by all the expected means—the Bible, prayer and meditation, participation in worship and communion, the fellowship of other Christians. I can't imagine our world without these orthodox means of grace, can you? Try it sometime. Suppose there were no church, no Bible, no teachers, no Christian fellowship. The world would be a bleak and desperate place, wouldn't it? What would our lives be like without them? What could we expect our children's lives to be like, and their children's after them?

The teachers are especially dear to my heart.

One of the most beautiful sights I ever saw was of a teacher and her students on the streets of Kyoto, Japan. The teacher was an instructor for the blind. All her children were lined up with white canes, awaiting their turns. One by one, she sent them on a course along the busy street, tap-tap-tapping as they went. They were learning to "see" and avoid the pitfalls of the street. I watched in fascination for half an hour. Whenever a child approached a pole or a fireplug or some other potential danger, I could see the teacher's body stiffen. She obviously wanted to rush forward and guide the child, to protect him or her from the unseen hazards of the environment. But she didn't. The children had to learn to see without her.

To me, it was a sacrament in motion, a picture of what all good teachers do. They teach us to see better. And then they stand back and watch as their students make their own mistakes.

How many eyes, through the years, Christ has anointed

through the concern of faithful teachers!

But Christ also touches our eyes through other means. It isn't only through teachers and the Bible and prayer that he touches us. He touches us in countless ways, many of which may seem to have little to do with religion. He touches us in nature, which is a wonderful place for learning to see. He touches us in art. The greatest theologian I ever studied under, Paul Tillich, once said that there is more spiritual depth in Vincent van Gogh's painting of old shoes than in any overtly religious painting in the world. Christ touches us in science. One of my students in divinity school a few years ago, an older man who had been a physicist, declared that he found more inspiration in astronomy and physics than in any book he had ever read or any sermon he had ever heard. Many find God in plays and movies and even on the Internet.

One of my quarrels with religious fundamentalism is the way it tries to restrict spiritual revelation to churches and religious teachings—especially its own. It champions the revelation of God in the Bible, the church, and church dogma, but ignores the wider vistas of revelation in art and culture outside the church. Fundamentalists are like the Pharisees of the Bible—they funnel all religious truth through their own narrow perceptual apparatus. Consequently their God, like that of the Pharisees, is only a caricature of the real God portrayed by the Bible, who is a God of mystery and transcendence, and cannot ever be captured in formulas or doctrines. The God of fundamentalism, despite all its display of devotion toward him, is really only an idol, and needs to be broken so that people are freed to worship the real God, the God beyond all that.

"The God beyond God," as Paul Tillich called him.

I remember an occasion shortly before Christmas when a student at Harvard Divinity School asked Dean Samuel H. Miller where he might attend church in New York during the holidays and be assured of having a significant religious experience. Dean Miller thought for a few seconds, then replied: "Well, I know one or two churches where you might have such an experience if the regular minister is not out of town." Then, after a brief pause, he added: "But I can give you the names of five or six plays on and off Broadway where I can guarantee such an experience, if you are willing to find it there."

That is what I mean. God is not limited to religious forms. Neither should our experience of God be limited to such forms. The world is not only the creation of God, it is the arena in which we see God. And it is only when our eyes are opened, and we begin to catch sight of God all around us, "like shining from shook foil," as Hopkins put it,[5] that we can speak of being saved. Any other view of salvation is simplistic and defective. We must *see* in order to be part of the kingdom.

I recall a little woman who could see beautifully. It was several years ago, and I was on a national committee to study the meaning of salvation in modern times. One of our meetings was at Rehoboth Beach, Delaware. We had spent the morning in discussions and the afternoon session had been entrusted to an artist named Walter Gaudnek. Walter was an explosive, dynamic kind of man who painted gigantic murals, unfurled great banners from airplanes, and experimented with videotape and movies. For that memorable afternoon in Delaware, he had planned what was then called a "happening," a dramatic event where the beginning was staged but was then allowed to flower into whatever form it chanced to.

5. Gerard Manley Hopkins, "God's Grandeur," in *Poems and Prose of Gerard Manley Hopkins* (Penguin. 1963), p. 27.

First, Walter loaded us into station wagons and took us to an old fishing harbor down the coast. There he had rented several dinghies and instructed us to row out into the harbor, circle our boats, and hold up some banners about salvation while he filmed the whole exercise on videotape. He had not counted on two things. One was that not many of us had ever managed a boat before, and on the whole we were very poor performers. The other was that Hurricane Agnes was bearing down on the East Coast of the U.S. and advance winds were already stirring the waters of the harbor into three- and four-foot waves.

"Get those banners up!" Walter shouted from the dock. "Keep your boats in a circle!"

But it was futile, for we could not manage the large dinghies in those churning waters. Our boats kept colliding with one another if we got near enough to form a circle. One man fell overboard and nearly drowned before we could rescue him. The old dockhands sitting beside the harbor looked on with mingled amusement and amazement at those strange antics from the inept sailors and the frustrated shouts of Walter Gaudnek.

After the debacle in the harbor, Walter packed us back into the station wagons and took us to a deserted beach house. It had obviously been deserted for years. If it had ever been painted, there was no remaining sign of it. But that was Walter's inspiration! He had brought dozens of partial cans of paint he had obtained from somewhere, and armed us with brushes and rollers and told us to paint the beach house. Soon there were people on the roof, people on the porch, and people all over the old house, splashing vivid colors on it to transform it into an art work. Two small boys bicycling past stopped to watch, and soon they too became involved in what we were doing. Walter had brought along a jazz saxophonist to play while we worked, and also a woman dressed in a leotard who danced on the rocks around us until she slipped and hurt her ankle. And of course Walter was busy videotaping the entire escapade.

That evening, when we entered a local seafood restaurant for dinner, we saw some of the old salts who had laughed at us by the harbor that afternoon. We felt as if we were some kind of weird celebrities!

After dinner, when we reassembled at the hotel, Walter set up a TV screen and played his video of our afternoon's activities for us to see. We laughed at the spectacle we had made and generally enjoyed the fun of it all. But one minister from New York City who had been invited to our discussions, Dr. James Forbes, who would later become the senior minister of famous Riverside Church, had been late in arriving, and it was he who asked, after we had viewed the video tapes, "What has all that got to do with salvation?"

Everyone fell silent before this question. I thought surely no one could really answer it. But someone did.

It was a little nun—I don't remember her name—who had been secundated to our group from the office of the National Council of Churches in New York. She had been very quiet until now. I don't recall that she had even spoken. But suddenly, in answer to Forbes' question, she became quite animated.

"Don't you see?" she said in a soft, gentle voice. "Before we came, that was an ordinary yacht harbor. The lives of the dockhands were humdrum and ordinary. They'll never forget this day. And that house! It was only a decaying old shack before we came and spread all that color around. Now it is an extraordinary place. Don't you see?! It *all* has to do with salvation!"

She saw, and she helped us to see.

That is what it's all about, isn't it? It's about seeing. It's about having our eyes opened to the glory of God all around us. It's about poetry and music and exaltation. It's about love and joy and dancing. It's about being anointed by Christ so that our daily existence is no longer ordinary but is always special. It's about being touched again and again, if necessary, until we have the heavenly vision, until we no longer see things hazily, as if we were nearsighted or farsighted, but see them with the kind of clarity that draws us into them and makes us part of God's divine wholeness.

The disciples in our previous text didn't see very well. But Jesus was able to anoint the eyes of a blind man—not once but twice—and make him see everything perfectly, the way we shall see when we are face to face with God.

Shh! Look, but Don't Tell!

Mark 8:27-9:13

Imagine you've just won a giant lottery. It's the best news you've had in years. But the operators of the lottery say, "Don't tell anybody you've won. We want it to remain a secret."

Suppose the mayor of your town comes to you and says, "The town council and I have just voted you the most important person in our community. We want to give you this medal as a token of our great esteem. There's only one provision. You mustn't tell anybody. It has to stay between you and us."

Let's pull out all the stops. Imagine you've been notified from Oslo that you're to be awarded the Nobel Peace Prize this year—possibly the most prestigious award in the world. Only, as in the other cases you've been asked to imagine, you are warned that you mustn't breathe a word of this award to anyone. It is to remain entirely secret.

There's a point to these suppositions, wild as they are. For this is essentially what happens to Jesus' disciples in our text.

First he asks them on their way to Caesarea Philippi who people are saying he is. They reply that there is speculation that he is the prophet Elijah or possibly another of the popular prophets of old come back to life.

"But who do *you* say that I am?" he presses them.

"You are the Messiah," says Peter.[1]

Right! Peter had given the correct answer, the one Jesus un-doubtedly hoped they would come up with.

But then he did a strange thing. The scripture says "he sternly ordered them not to tell anyone about him."[2]

All this time, through all the adventures they'd had to-gether, and after he had scolded them for having eyes but not seeing and ears but not hearing, they showed some intelligence and indicated that they really did know he was the Messiah, the Savior from God, and he told them to put a lid on it and not tell anybody.

What a strange order!

A few days later, Jesus took Peter, James, and John, his most intimate friends, into "a high mountain apart," where "he was transfigured before them."[3] "His clothes became dazzling white," says the scripture, "such as no one on earth could bleach them."[4] Isn't that a fascinating description? Can you imagine a contest among the various bleach and whitening companies to see if they could duplicate this remarkable effect?

And there was more.

Elijah and Moses, the two most popular and widely known figures in Hebrew history, appeared to Jesus and talked with him while he was in that dazzling state. The great prophet and the great law-giver were seen visiting with the rabbi that Peter and his confreres had already identified as God's Messiah.

Peter's impulsive reaction was understandable.

"Rabbi," he exclaimed, "it is good for us to be here; let us make three dwellings, one for you, one for Moses, and one for Elijah"[5]—three tabernacles, or residences like the ones the Jews constructed for God during their years of wilderness wander-

1. Mark 8:27-29.
2. Mark 8:30.
3. Mark 9:2.
4. Mark 9:3.
5. Mark 9:5.

ings.

The scripture says he really didn't know what he should say under the circumstances because he, like the others, was completely terrified. I understand that, don't you? It must have been like having an alien spaceship land right beside you and suck you up into an incredibly bright interior and an experience you'd never dreamed of having.

Then came the climax.

An eerie cloud overshadowed them, and out of the cloud came the unmistakable voice of God. "This is my Son, the Beloved," it said; "listen to him!"[6] And it was over. The cloud was gone. Elijah was gone. Moses was gone. There was no more voice. Only Jesus and his disciples remained.

"Boy!" thought the disciples as they started back down the mountain, "wait till we see the others and tell them! They won't believe it!"

But then, just as he had done before, Jesus cut across the path of their natural reaction and ordered that none of them should tell anyone about what they had witnessed.

The veil of secrecy again. The zipped lips.

What was going on?!

That's a good question. Scholars have been trying to answer it for centuries. "The Messianic Secret," they call it. Jesus' order that his followers shouldn't tell anyone who he was or what he had done.

Why? Why should he do that?

The most common answer is that he didn't want to provoke his enemies any more than he already had and didn't want such large crowds around him that he couldn't complete his mission. His mission, it is commonly thought, was to die on the cross

---

6. Mark 9:7.

for the sins of the world. If it became widespread knowledge that he was the Messiah, such hordes of people would gather around him and be so protective of him that his enemies could not hope to destroy him.

No silence, no cross.

There's another possibility. It's a long shot, but it's still a possibility. If the Gospel of Mark was indeed a Gnostic document, then there is the Gnostic code of mystery to be considered. I have mentioned it before. Gnostic Christians, like their counterparts in other mystery religions of the time, preferred to guard their sacred rites and beliefs from common usage, believing that anything bruited about too freely would lose its power, its cachet, its special nature. They kept their greatest insights and expressions of faith for rehearsal inside the community.

Whatever the reason for Jesus' enjoining the disciples to silence, it seems odd to us because our instincts would lead us to do exactly the opposite, and race around telling everyone we knew that Jesus was the Messiah and we had received confirmation of that fact by a transcendent experience with him. It's human nature. Surely almost anyone would wish to tell others about something like this!

But perhaps there is some kind of lesson here about how we should handle our religious experience.

Do you remember the Myers-Briggs typology chart, and all the other ways of classifying our personalities and how we will typically behave under certain circumstances? Some people are classified as Introverts and others as Extraverts, and a whole series of reactions are affected by that simple fact alone.

If the disciples with Jesus had been introverts, for example, it would have been much easier for them to follow his instructions not to tell anyone. They would have internalized their experience and quietly meditated on it for the remainder of their lives. Extraverts, on the other hand, would have been beside themselves to tell what had happened. They would have wanted to share it immediately with others, for they wouldn't have known how to handle it any other way.

Current Christianity—the religion of our own day—is essentially divisible into the same two camps, isn't it? Some Christians are quiet, thoughtful, meditative—they like to ponder their religious experience and are often loath to talk about it publicly—while other Christians are open, expressive, and want to blurt out to the world what has happened to them, proclaiming Jesus the Lord of their lives before everyone they know.

The former tend to join the Episcopal or Unitarian churches, and perhaps even the Presbyterian church. The latter are most often found among Baptists, Methodists, and various sectarian churches.

Sometimes we aren't appreciative enough of this division in what our personalities are like, and tend to speak ill of Christians who don't react to or talk about their religious experience the way we do.

The majority of Christians are of the demonstrative sort. But perhaps this text in Mark reminds us of the value of being introspective about our faith—of quietly and unobtrusively pondering the presence of God and what it means to our total existence. Here were the disciples almost bursting to tell others about what they knew and had experienced, and yet they had to suppress it and tell no one. Didn't that make their experience even more intense, forcing them to internalize what they had seen and felt instead of dissipating the aura of it by going out and speaking of what had happened?

Let's imagine a somewhat parallel situation. Suppose a very important person—say, the president of our country—were to call you in and tell you some things about what he was going to do in the near future, and then told you not to mention these things to anyone. How would you feel? Wouldn't you feel the burden of the confidence even more keenly than if you could rush out and tell someone what you had been told? Wouldn't you watch every announcement from the White House with very keen interest to see if the president was acting on the things of which he had spoken to you? In the end, you would be a deeper, more intense person for having internalized the whole experience, for not having divulged it to others as if you were a mere pipeline for the news.

It's difficult to be sure, but this may have been part of the dynamic involved in the way the messianic secret was handled by Mark. The very air of secrecy enhances the sense of mystery and transcendence we feel in reading his Gospel. We are reminded by it that something very special was happening in the coming of Christ—something to which we should be extraordinarily sensitive and alert, straining all of our senses to apprehend and respond to it.

I once had a parishioner who seldom took communion because she wanted it to remain extremely sacred to her. She said that if she took it more often she might lose the sense of awe and holiness she felt in taking it. Her hands actually trembled when she did receive the bread and cup. This is what I mean by the sensitivity inculcated by the secrecy in the Gospel. The news of Jesus' messiahship is not allowed to become vulgar or common. It remains what it was intended to be: an incredible recognition of the highest order!

I recall part of an absurdist play I read years ago, Tom Stoppard's *Rosencrantz and Guildenstern Are Dead*. The play is a kind of footnote to Shakespeare's *Hamlet*, in which both Rosencrantz and Guildenstern were minor characters. The theme of the play, if it can be summarized so briefly, has to do with the banality of human existence—the way even the highest experiences of our lives get reduced to pedestrian or inconsequential status.

At one point in the play, Guildenstern—Guil, as Stoppard calls him—tells the Parable of the Unicorn. It is about two men walking along when one of them sees a unicorn cross the road ahead of them. He sees it, but it hardly registers, for he can think of several reasons why he may not have actually beheld what he thought he beheld.

Suddenly, though, his friend says, "My God, I must be dreaming, I thought I saw a unicorn!"

At this point, says Guil, the experience of the two men becomes as stunning and gripping as it will ever be, for each has corroborated the experience of the other.

For there to be a third or fourth or sixth man to have the same experience and thus further corroborate what the first two saw would only water down the experience, make it common and dull for all of them. Soon, says Guil, there would be a crowd of people exclaiming, "Look, look! A horse with an arrow in its forehead! It must have been mistaken for a deer."[7]

It all has to do with how we deal with our own perceptions. The Sufi religion, in particular, has a lot to say about finding

7. Tom Stoppard, *Rosencrantz and Guildenstern Are Dead* (Faber & Faber, 1967), pp. 14-15.

the extraordinary in the ordinary—in our own breathing, in a cup of tea, in the sound of a woodpecker on a dead tree. It is a matter of truly seeing things, something Mark's Gospel is about, and realizing we are in the presence of the holy. Unfortunately, most of us never develop a talent for seeing and feeling. We go through life without realizing that, as Michael Mayne, a former dean of Westminster Cathedral in London, once put it, "Epiphanies, if we did but know it, lie like unopened gifts at every turn of the road and every stage of our journey."[8]

The converse is unfortunately true—that our epiphanies or discoveries of God can be dulled, muted, or obliterated by treating them too commonly, by becoming so familiar with them that they no longer have the power to thrill or captivate us.

This is why I say we might learn something from Mark's emphasis on Jesus' admonition to secrecy. There are areas of Christianity where the celebrations of God in Christ are so formulaic and insistent that any sense of God's actual presence is all but cancelled out. I have been in religious services where the language and hymnody were so exuberant and repetitive that they seemed to take the place of God, not to evoke any real sense of what Rudolf Otto called the Wholly Other. It was as if God had been there at one time and the remembrance of that experience had become so ritualized and concretized that absolutely no one could possibly make a similar discovery again, for the present worship all but prevented it.

This is a problem for any organized religion. The experience invariably loses something in translation. From the time Christianity began to have councils to discuss its faith, the faith began to be diminished. Instead of the immediacy of the expe-

8. Michael Mayne, *This Sunrise of Wonder* (HarperCollins/Fount, 1995), p. 53.

rience, people received social and logical assurance of the existence of God. The fact was distilled into an idea, and the idea might or might not have any real potency. It was now subject to debate, categorization, and examination by committee. And how many committees have ever achieved a theophany?

As James P. Carse says, "Using words to isolate some portion of the flux [of life] is like taking a photograph of the surface of the ocean. No sooner does the lens close than a different ocean appears. It may be the same ocean but no single photograph, or any number of photographs, can capture its oneness."[9]

So much, then, for creeds and theologies and philosophical reflections on Christianity. So much, even, for sermons and testimonies. It is possible to lose the real in the very act of attempting to recreate it!

I believe this is what Mark was trying to say in his Gospel—that what happened in Jesus was so magical, so transcendent, so mysterious, that any attempt to reduce it to words or images——even to a confession like Peter's in behalf of the disciples—is futile, or, worse, tantamount to losing what the first Christians were trying to express.

I could be wrong. This might not have been in Mark's mind at all. But what if it was? Suppose he was actually trying to warn us about the dangers of institutionalizing the gospel. Wouldn't it be cavalier of us to dismiss such a warning without due consideration?

Poets will understand this, for they deal daily in the relation of words to inspiration. They know it is a fragile relationship, easily violated or broken. So they tread lightly, listen carefully, try to maintain a vital sensitivity to the aura of what they are doing, the emanations of the process and not just the

9. James P. Carse, *Breakfast at the Victory* (HarperSanFrancisco, 1994), p. 24.

thing in itself. Even modern physics supports such a thesis. We know that the location of an electron is changed by merely shining a light on it in order to observe it. The light literally knocks the electron off course. And the same is true of the religious experience——we alter it by attempting to define, ritualize, or concretize it. It is too fragile, too volatile, to endure our attempts at capturing it.

So where does this leave us? With a choice between a religion fully ritualized and documented, on one hand, and, on the other, one still inchoate, in progress, never fully zipped up or nailed down. For myself, I shall take the latter kind, and pray that in my last days I shall still be seeking a more immediate understanding and looking for the extraordinary in the ordinary.

If I am reading Mark correctly, I believe he was saying that being able to *see*—to obtain an insight even for a moment—is enough to reorder our lives, to transform everything. This is why the stories about calming the sea and this narrative about transfiguration are so important. They represent those peak experiences in which we suddenly and irrevocably recognize Jesus as *Lord*—the ones when we know that life is more than its sheer physicality and realize that God is here among us!

All three are post-resurrection stories—parables about what it means to recognize Jesus as a holy, living presence in the very midst of our ordinary, everyday existence.

And this is the good news, the gospel of Jesus Christ!

A Big Lesson about Little People

Mark 10:13-16

I was tempted to begin this sermon with references to the way children often say big or redemptive things to the adults in their lives. Like the little boy who says to his dad when he sees him in a tuxedo, "Dad, you shouldn't wear that. You know you always have a headache the next morning when you do." Or the little girl who saw a pressed leaf fall out of her Sunday school teacher's Bible and said, "Oh, you just lost Adam's underwear!"

That might have been cute, but it would have been cheap, because this text isn't about how smart kids are and what clever things they can say.

It's about two things.

The first is compassion. Jesus cared about children. His culture didn't. We see that from the way the disciples acted. They were brusque to the children and told them to stay away from Jesus. And they were brusque because that was the way people treated children in that era. Take the Ten Commandments. They have a rule for how children were supposed to honor and obey their parents, but no rule about how parents were supposed to treat children.

So, just as Mark's Jesus treated women with respect in an era when most people didn't, Jesus regarded children with tender care when those around him didn't. He rebuked the disciples for their callousness toward little ones and gathered the little ones around him as if they were special. He single-handedly changed the way the world has regarded children. It took some centuries to do it, but he was the one who started it.

One of the results came to me recently in the form of a photograph e-mailed by a friend. It showed Sergeant John Gebhart of the United States Air Force asleep in a chair holding a small brown-skinned girl of perhaps three or four years as she slept snuggly in his arms. The explanation was terse. It said only that her family had been executed—probably in Afghanistan—and she had been shot in the head. The wound was still quite visible on the back of her skull She was afraid and cried except when she was in Gebhart's arms. So he had held her and they had slept in that position for the past four nights. The big American soldier and the little girl who probably couldn't even speak his language.

When I saw it, I thought of Jesus' words to his disciples: "Let the little children come to me."[1] I could imagine an invisible line drawn from Jesus to Sergeant Gebhart.

The second thing the text is about is the kingdom of God and who can actually get into it. And from a gospel writer's viewpoint, this must be even more important than showing how children ought to be treated. It is, in a sense, a theological statement. Just as Mark spoke volumes by having blind people recognize the Savior, in this little vignette about Jesus and the children he was saying what kind of people actually understand the nature of God's heavenly kingdom.

1. Mark 10:14.

The disciples, the men who were with Jesus day and night for months if not years, the ones who should have known and understood beyond everybody else, were blind, deaf, and thick-headed. Even after they had finally figured out that, strange as it was, he was somehow the promised Savior of Israel, they still faltered, for it was only a half-understanding, and not enough to prevent their bolting when he was crucified.

Similarly in every age there have been people who should know who Jesus really was and what his coming meant to the world—scholars, preachers, bishops, people of repute and quality—but are only partially convinced. With all the evidence before them and generations of faith behind them, they still hesitate and falter, unwilling to forget everything to follow him.

As Jesus is quoted in the Gnostic document *The Sophia of Jesus Christ,* "I want you to know that all men born on earth from the foundation of the world until now, being dust, while they have inquired about God, who he is and what he is like, have not found him. Now the wisest among them have speculated from the ordering of the world and (its) movement. But their speculation has not reached the truth."[2]

The little children, on the other hand, are different. Their faith in the one who beckons them and dawdles them on his knee is complete and unwavering. They accept him for who he is and enter totally into the relationship he offers, holding nothing back, seeking nothing for themselves beyond the moment of their experience. There is no speculating about the nature of anything. There is no feigning or calculating about what they shall get out of it. They are simply there and enter into a symbiotic relationship with him, a union that is in and of itself, without reference to anything beyond it.

2. *The Nag Hammadi Library in English,* p. 223.

The Gnostics frequently spoke of Jesus and the Pleroma, the fullness of everything. In their thinking, we all come from the Pleroma when we are born, but begin to lose our sense of the fullness until we are reclaimed by God and reintroduced to our sense of the Pleroma. Then we struggle to know it more and more—to repossess the heavenly knowledge—and, if we are among the fortunate ones, reenter it through the mystery of Christ.

A paragraph in *The Tripartite Tractate* reveals the spirit of this mystery:

> The Logos established him(self) at first, when he beautified the Totalities, as a basic principle and cause and ruler of the things which came to be, like the Father, the one who was the cause of the establishment, which was the first to exist after him. He created the pre-existent images, which he brought forth in thanks and glorification. Then he beautified the place of those whom he had brought forth in glory, which is called "Paradise" and "the Enjoyment" and the Joy full of sustenance" and "the Joy," which pre-exist.[3]

Children, the Gnostics believed, retain more of a sense of this Logos, of paradise and natural joy, than adults. Their souls have not yet become so contaminated by worldly cares, greed, ambition, and great design as those of their elders. Therefore they are nearer in nature to Christ, and it was reasonable for Jesus to say "it is to such as these (i.e., the children) that the kingdom of God belongs."[4]

Interestingly, the Gnostic *Gospel of Thomas* contains a saying of Jesus very similar to the one in Mark:

3. Ibid., p. 83.
4. Mark 10:14.

> Jesus saw infants being suckled. He said to his
> disciples, "These infants being suckled are like
> those who enter the kingdom."
>   They said to him, "Shall we then, as children,
> enter the kingdom?"
>   Jesus said to them, "When you make the two
> one, and when you make the inside like the outside
> and the outside like the inside, and the above like
> the below, and when you make the male and the fe-
> male one and the same, so that the male not be
> male nor the female female; and when you fashion
> eyes in place of an eye, and a hand in place of a
> hand, and a foot in place of a foot, and a likeness
> in place of a likeness; then will you enter [the king-
> dom]."[5]

Here the obvious characterization of childhood is of a time
when we have not yet begun to differentiate among things, or
to divide the world into this and that and the other. Everything
is still whole to the child. It is still a part of everything else.
Small children don't even recognize differences in sexuality;
they "make the male and the female one and the same." They
don't even know wise from unwise, for they are unconscious of
their own wholeness.

So the real goal of life, to Mark and the Gnostics, is the return to unification, the growing once more into the guileless-
ness and nondifferentiation of little children, so that everything
may be whole again, for the wholeness *is* the Pleroma, the fullness of everything. It is the state of innocent joy and content-
ment, like that of the little children Jesus takes into his arms
and blesses. They are the models to Jesus' disciples and to all

5. *The Nag Hammadi Library in English*, p. 129.

adults. Therefore Jesus said: "Truly I tell you, whoever does not receive the kingdom of God as a little child will never enter it."[6]

If there was ever a child that embodied the picture of the young heavenly citizen that Jesus spoke about, it must have been Matthew Stepanek—Mattie—who in his fourteen years of life became one of the greatest ambassadors for peace and sharing this world has ever known. Mattie had a rare form of muscular dystrophy, and spent most of his life in a motorized wheelchair with a portable oxygen tank. He was only a slight little boy who wore glasses and spoke like a quizzical little adult. But he won hearts wherever he went, he published several books of poems, and he was one of the greatest ambassadors of love and generosity who ever lived. President Jimmy Carter, who was his friend and spoke at his funeral in June 2004, said of Mattie: "He was still a boy, although he had the mind and the consciousness and the awareness of global affairs of a mature, philosophical adult."

You probably remember some of his beautiful poems, which he often quoted on *Oprah* or *Larry King Live* or other programs where he was interviewed and which are available in the several best-selling books he published. Here are a few lines from a poem called "For Our World," which encapsulate his extraordinary wisdom and the spirit of love and acceptance that characterized his thought:

> In many ways, we are the same.
> Our differences are unique treasures.
> We have, we are, a mosaic of gifts
> To nurture, to offer, to accept.
> We need to be.
> Just be.[7]

6. Mark 10:15.
7. Matthew Stepanek, *Hope Through Heartsongs* (Hyperion, 2002).

Mattie was eleven years old when he wrote those lines.

He wrote a poem about what it would be like to die and go to heaven. He said to God that he tried to imagine it, and wondered if God would extend his right hand to him. Then he wondered if God would extend his left hand. But then the answer came to him: God would extend both of his hands, for his arms would be wide open to welcome him.

Isn't this what Jesus was talking about when he said that we have to be like children to enter the kingdom of heaven? He was only a boy, an undersized, underdeveloped, handicapped child. But he had a heart as big as all outdoors, and wanted to see the whole world enveloped in love and joy. He wanted people to be open and tolerant and forgiving. He wanted the poor to eat as well as the rich, and for everybody to live in heartfelt acceptance of everybody else.

Maybe he was an extraordinary child. But he cared about all the others who were ordinary, and wanted to meet them in heaven, where they would all join hands and dance around the throne of God.

Jesus knew what he was talking about, didn't he?

Wanting It Both Ways

Mark 10:17-31

I understand the man in this text, don't you? He's like a lot of good people I've known in the churches I pastored. In any lineup, they had the most to offer—good positions, plenty of money, attractive personalities, nice clothes, spotless backgrounds, and a willingness to consider alternatives. They were usually the people who ended up on the church's major boards and committees—movers and shakers, people with the substance to understand whatever issues arose, an ability to consider things and make sound decisions. They were the ones I enjoyed having lunch with at their clubs or sitting across from at dinner parties. In short, they were the most attractive people in town, the ones everybody agreed were fun, companionable, and influential.

But ... and here I should draw a line across the page and provide the flip side to what I have been saying about them.

There was almost always one thing about them that both-ered me, that gnawed at the underside of my consciousness like a small rodent trying to get out of a box. I seldom admitted it and tried to not even think about it. But, like the man in Mark's narrative, they would almost never take a big risk with who they were and what they had. Only rarely would one of them step across the line toward any position that seemed like a gamble. They had learned to be cautious about the future, to hedge their bets on almost any issue, and not to be the first to appear radical or daring.

Sometimes, in a board or committee meeting, I would secretly wish for one of them to break ranks with the others and say something that would demand real discipleship of all of us, that would challenge us to move beyond our margins of safety and lay everything on the line for Jesus. Oh, they were on Jesus' side. Nobody ever questioned that. It was part of their CV as church leaders and respectable members of our society. But they almost never erred on the side of spontaneity or of risking something for the kingdom of God.

Which brings us back to the wealthy man in our text.

He was polite. He was more than polite, he was friendly and outgoing. "Good Teacher," he called Jesus. Which immediately put Jesus on the defensive. "Why do you call me good?" he said. "No one is good but God alone."[1]

Ah, we want to quibble, Jesus only *said* that. Everyone knows he was divine. Why did he tell the man that only God is good? Was he trying to elicit a confession from the man acknowledging him as God?

Well, no, frankly.

The Gospel of Mark doesn't equate Jesus with God. In the Gnostic tradition, it regarded Jesus as God Manifest, not God Incarnate. Jesus was the Son of Man, the Son of David, the Messiah, but not God. If that bothers us, then we should take it up with Mark or rethink our own Christology. This is a Christology older than that of the historical church councils and our creeds.

---

1. Mark 10:18.

The man wanted eternal life.

He knew what he must do, said Jesus—he had the commandments. And Jesus referred to some of them—not mur-
dering, not committing adultery, not stealing, not bearing false
witness, not defrauding. Plus one positive commandment—
honoring father and mother.

Eagerly, the man replied, "Teacher, I have kept all these
since my youth."[2] He must have thought he had already won
the prize, and was waiting for Jesus to acknowledge it.

The text says Jesus looked at him and loved him.

There must have been something special about the man,
something comely or fetching. We know people who are almost
instantly lovable. Many of the people of whom I spoke earlier,
our best church members, are like that. Their personalities are
warm and magnetic. They invite love and care.

But, as in the case of our church members, there was something missing.

"You lack one thing," Jesus said; "go, sell what you have, and
give the money to the poor, and you will have treasure in
heaven; then come, follow me."[3]

Ah! That was the testing point, wasn't it? He was a good
man. He was a lovable man. And he was eager for the kingdom
of God. But he had this one last hurdle to jump, this one big
question to settle: Was he willing to give up everything for the
kingdom and become one of Jesus' itinerant followers?

You know the sad story: he wasn't.

Mark says the man was "shocked" by Jesus' imposition of
this requirement. He was stunned at the realization that what
he had done and was doing was not enough. He bridled at the
thought of giving away everything he had. It was too much to

2. Mark 10:20.
3. Mark 10:21-22.

ask. Jesus had no right!

Or did he?

That's the sticking point for most of us, isn't it? And for all those nice, attractive people we work with on our boards and committees. We all want it both ways. We want to go on being good and keeping the commandments and serving the Lord in our modest ways *and* we want to be on good terms with Jesus. We even want to think we are following him. We don't want to think of anything as radical as what Jesus demanded of the rich man. We want to go on as we are *and* to regard ourselves as his followers.

Oh my, it does test us, doesn't it?

The man in the text went away "grieving," says Mark, "for he had many possessions."[4]

Ah, that's us all right. We too have many possessions. They aren't all monetary. Some have to do with our families, our neighborhoods, our jobs, our standing in the community, and other somewhat intangible properties. The point is, we want to remain as we are—comfortable in our own skins, comfortable with our identities, comfortable with our situations.

Was there anything about Jesus' demand that has more significance when seen from a gnostic perspective than when it is regarded as a merely evangelical text the way we've always heard it preached? Well, yes. Perhaps. For the Gnostic, seeing, knowing, gaining the insight was supposed to transform a person. It left him or her totally different from before. It was like stepping out of the old identity into a completely new one, as if one had walked through a doorway from a dark room into one that was brilliantly lit, so that everything—*everything*—was viewed differently.

4. Mark 10:22.

So the man in our text was not merely an example of the comfortable Israelites who weren't prepared to become itinerant followers of Jesus because it might make them less comfortable. He was a paradigm of those who did not yet know—who didn't yet have the *gnosis*—and therefore turned back from being Jesus' followers or lacked the insight to take that final step into real transcendence.

Our old understanding of the story was dramatic enough. But this understanding is *super*dramatic. It is the old understanding squared or carried to the infinite degree. Now it should glow in our consciousness, or flash like a great neon sign beckoning us onward and upward to the point where we abandon our former comforts—everything that contributed to our sense of security as we were—and really become followers of Jesus.

I don't know if you've considered it, but we live in a transitional age when globalism is fast becoming a major factor in how we behave and respond to everything. Following Jesus has a lot more possibilities for all of us today than it held even fifty years ago. It can mean working with displaced people in New Orleans or becoming a teacher in New York's Bowery district or serving Christ on a college campus—all of which I have friends who are doing. It can take us to Africa to work with survivors of genocide or Italy to care for street orphans or Houston to assist families dealing with cancer or almost anywhere on earth to become transformational agents of love and healing.

Bruce Kennedy and his wife Karleen are among these modern followers of Jesus. Bruce, at 52, was president of Alaska Airlines, earning half a million dollars a year. He and Karleen were members of a Presbyterian church and were on a weekend retreat when they felt invited to follow Christ in some special way. Alaska Airlines was booming under Bruce's leadership, earning more than a billion dollars a year. But he felt a higher calling.

"We decided our time of stewardship of Alaska Airlines was coming to an end," he said, "and decided to give the company back to the Lord and trust him to lead us to some new endeavor."

Their calling, they decided, was to the Third World. They moved to a village called Wei Fang, 270 miles southeast of Beijing, China, where they worked as English teachers in exchange for a modest home and a couple of bicycles to get around on.

Bruce and Karleen are part of a growing number of Americans who are serving Jesus on the other side of the world and trying to build bridges of hope between other countries and ours. It is a mission of peace and love, they believe, and they are gladly sacrificing more comfortable lifestyles at home to serve God in villages where there are not any Walmarts, Pizza Huts, or even, in some cases, running water and electricity.

This is what Mark's little story is about. It is about stepping into the light, and knowing Jesus in a way that makes all one's former dependencies and attachments obsolete. The rich ruler wasn't able to do it. Most of us and our fellow church members can't do it either. But for those who can it is a passport to the most important thing in the world!

A Kingdom Beyond Ambition

Mark 10:35-45

Most of us don't like pushy, ambitious people, do we? I think of an associate minister I once knew. When he joined our staff, he seemed as humble and self-effacing as a young minister ought to be. But he soon began to exhibit signs of deep, burning ambition. He invariably maneuvered for assignments that would give him the best chance of impressing others. He had a way of seeming to deny credit for what he did while actually encouraging others to heap it on him. In subtle ways, he undermined the credibility and standing of fellow staff members. He ingratiated himself with the most important people in the congregation, then used their friendship to promote himself in every conceivable way. I imagined his getting up in the morning and making a list of all the little things he would do that day to shine a spotlight on himself and his talents as a minister.

Somehow I get the feeling that James and John might have been like this young minister. At least they appear in that light in this text. Curiously, Matthew says in his Gospel that James' and John's mother was the one who asked the favor that they might sit on either side of Jesus when he came into his glory.[1] If Matthew followed Mark's Gospel in many instances, as most scholars believe, this would have been an odd bit of information

1. Matthew 20:20-28.

to add. Perhaps Matthew was attempting to divert the guilt associated with the request from the disciples themselves and blame it on their mother. The two men were, after all, prominent figures in the early church.

If they really did say, as Mark reports, "Grant us to sit, one at your right hand and one at your left, in your glory,"[2] then they hadn't understood anything Jesus had said to them after the rich ruler went away. "Many who are first," he had told them, "will be last, and the last will be first."[3] It hadn't registered with them that the kingdom was not about getting ahead. Jesus had warned them that he must die an unpleasant death before being raised to new life,[4] and apparently they thought that when this happened he would come into his glory, his fulfillment as the Messiah. They were merely putting in their bid for favorable positions when he did.

When the other disciples realized that James and John were trying to steal a march on them, they were unhappy.

So Jesus used their disgruntlement as a teaching opportunity. "You know that among the Gentiles those whom they recognize as their rulers lord it over them, and their great ones are tyrants over them," he said.[5] Every Jew knew this. They had seen the strictness of the Romans who occupied their country, and how rank was everything to them. "But this isn't the way it should be with you," said Jesus. "Whoever wishes to become great among you must be your servant"[6]—he must become a *slave*, which is what the Greek literally says. That was what he himself had become, said Jesus. He had come among them "not to be served but to serve."[7]

2. Mark 10:37.
3. Mark 10:31.
4. Mark 10:34.
5. Mark 10:42.
6. Mark 10:43.
7. Mark 10:40.

How ashamed James and John must have been when they heard the Master say this! I would have been, wouldn't you? And their shame must have increased exponentially through the years as they realized more and more what it meant to be part of the kingdom of God, which is completely unlike human kingdoms where such orders exist.

In the tradition of the Christian Gnostics, God was often conceived as the Pleroma, the Fullness, the Totality of All That Is. When one became a believer, a "knower," one entered into that fullness with God. It was like stepping out of darkness into light, out of mere earthly knowledge and perception into an entirely higher level of knowing and perceiving. It was, in fact, merging with the Totality itself.

James and John's request to sit in places of honor, then, was indicative of their lower stage of understanding. They had not yet progressed in their knowledge and understanding of the kingdom to the point where they would understand the foolishness of such a petition. Jesus said it was not his to give them what they asked. That was a gentle way of upbraiding them for their as-yet lack of knowing. Eventually they would see and understand. But for now they were still in the dark, still acting out of their unenlightened selves, still craving what most people wanted in life, to sit in places of honor and be recognized as important personalities.

Years ago, I was the speaker for National Armed Forces Day at the National Cathedral in Washington, DC. All of us who would be participating in the chancel—several chaplains from the various divisions of the Armed Forces, a couple of dignitaries from the State Department, some bishops and archbishops of the Episcopalian Church, and two or three people from the staff of the cathedral—gathered in the vestry a few minutes before the service. When we received the word that we should line up for the procession during the opening hymn, there was some confusion as we tried to find our proper places. As the speaker, I was to proceed just ahead of the local archbishop.

I do not remember the archbishop's name—seriously—but do recall that he was very impressed by his own importance. He had an imperiousness about him that derived more from earthly pride than from any heavenly authority. And when the bishop or dean of the cathedral—I don't recall which it was— fell quietly into line between me and the archbishop, the archbishop barked an order: "So-and-So [using the man's last name without a title], you don't belong there! Get up closer to the front!"

It was a small thing, but the memory of it has lingered in my mind all these years as a blotch on the beauty and pageantry of the day. It made me wonder about the depth of spirituality in a man who would treat one of his subordinates so rudely in front of all of us who were assembled there to honor the men and women of the nation's Armed Forces. Who did he think he was, this popinjay with his beautiful robes and golden mitre?! Wasn't he aware, for all his ecclesiastical eminence, of the nature of God's kingdom and the reminder of Jesus that whoever would be first in it must be the servant of all? I was embarrassed at his lack of understanding—the same lack that Jesus observed in his disciples when they sought to sit in the places of honor.

I set beside that memory the image of Mother Teresa, a saintly woman who for all her prayer and absorption in God never forgot that she was a servant of the poorest of the poor. Once, according to reporter Courtney Tower, a priest approached Mother Teresa at a conference they were both attending and complained to her, "Mother, the poor lord it over us." Mother Teresa looked back at him and said, "The poor *are* our Lord."[8]

We are not all Mother Teresas, of course, and cannot match the level of her saintliness. But we can at least aspire to be more like her and thus become a blessing to God's little ones whom we encounter every day.

A friend recently e-mailed me a story that beguiles me. It was about three businessmen rushing through an airport to catch their planes and get home at the end of the day. As they ran through the corridor, one bumped into a small vendor's stand where a girl was selling apples and knocked it over, sending the apples flying in all directions. He murmured an apology but kept on running. One of his friends also plunged ahead. The third man beheld the dismayed girl and the mess they had made, and stopped to help.

"If I miss the plane," he called to his friends, "tell my wife I'll be home as soon as I can."

He resurrected the tipped-over stand and began picking up apples. While he was doing this, he saw that the girl was groping around on the floor and it suddenly dawned on him that she was blind. When he had helped recover the fruit, he apologized that some of them were too badly bruised to sell. Taking out his billfold, he handed her two twenty-dollar bills and said he hoped that would take care of it. He patted her hand and started off to find a ticket agent and see if he could get a later flight.

8. Courtney Tower, "Mother Teresa's Work of Grace," *Reader's Digest*, December 1987, p. 248.

The girl's voice followed him as he turned away. "Mister," she asked, "are you Jesus?"

He wasn't, of course. But wasn't it great that she associated what he did with Jesus? Wouldn't you like to live in such a way that people associate you with him?

Maybe that's what Jesus wanted James and John to understand. The way to the top is to start at the bottom—and to stay there forever if necessary!

What the Blind Man Saw

Mark 10:46-52

Writers have always been fascinated by the extraordinary compensatory gifts of those who are blind. Tiresias, the sightless soothsayer of the *Odyssey*, for example, was the subject of a number of strange and interesting stories. In one of them, he happened upon the goddess Athena in her bath, and she blinded him as a punishment. When his mother pled with her to undo her curse, she was unable to do it, but changed his hearing in such a way that he was able to understand the birds as they talked. In another story, he saw two snakes copulating and struck at them; as a punishment, he was changed into a woman for seven years, so that he had not only male understanding but female understanding as well.

My wife and I have a friend who has been blind since early adulthood. We often forget that she is blind, for she acts very much like a person who isn't. She often takes walks without her seeing-eye dog, and when she goes out to dinner she feeds herself so faultlessly that not even the waiter notices anything different about her. Once, she said to my wife, "That is a beautiful red dress." My wife, astounded, said, "Who told you it is red?" "Oh, I could feel it," she said. "Red emits more heat than other colors." Many times she has amazed us with her ability to see and hear things that ordinary people miss.

We don't know exactly what Mark thought about Bartimaeus, the blind man whose story he tells in this passage. Perhaps he too had unusual wisdom and insight to compensate for his lack of vision. But as Mark doesn't comment on this we are left to suppose that for him the real point of Bartimaeus' sudden awareness—that the man who was passing near him in his darkness was Christ, the Messiah anointed by God—is that Bartimaeus, a man with unseeing eyes, was given to see and understand what all the sighted people around him could not.

This is, after all, the tension throughout this remarkable Gospel, a tension between those who can see the truth about Jesus' real nature and those who can't. It runs like a broad river through the nature of the disciples themselves, who most of the time, despite their familiarity with Jesus, fail to see or understand who he really is. "Why are you afraid?" he asks them after he has calmed a storm at sea. "Have you still no faith?"[1] "Do you have eyes," he asked them later, "and fail to see? Do you have ears, and fail to hear?"[2]

The marginal people in society often see what others cannot, don't they? Servants know what their masters cannot understand. Tenants see things property owners cannot comprehend. The poor and outcast possess a wisdom the rich and comfortable lack.

I remember Dorothy Cooper, a homeless woman who attended our church in Los Angeles. She was a slightly overweight woman about sixty with eyes that penetrated like laser beams. She often carried an autoharp and stopped to strum it and sing a song. "Blue Hawaii" was one of her favorites.

1. Mark 4:40.
2. Mark 8:10.

Dorothy didn't have to be homeless. She was intelligent and clever, and could easily have held a good job. But she preferred to be free, wafting here and there like the wind. Some nights, when the weather was warm, she slept in the parks. Other times, she rented a room in a seedy old hotel. And when she did that, she frequently took friends with her so they would be warm.

Despite her strange life, she had an unusual amount of wisdom. She understood about love and generosity. She had tender feelings for those who had suffered. I often thought that if she had lived in the time of Jesus she might easily have become one of his disciples, for she lived very much as he did and said the kind of things he would have liked.

This is one of the great anomalies of Mark's Gospel. Those who are most educated and possess the greatest status and wealth often remain blind and unseeing, while those who appear to be deprived—the Bartimaeuses of the world—are the ones with the real gift of sightedness. They are able to receive the staggering truth of Jesus' messiahship—of God's transcendent power in the world—when others can't.

It is a mystery, isn't it? In fact, the Gospel is about mystery. It is about tensions and anomalies and contradictions and irreconcilable differences. It is about the way God is working in the world and the fact that most of us never have a clue, never understand what it is all about, because we are too much into ourselves, too proud of our intellectualism, too cocksure of our way of knowing things.

Years ago, I heard a story told by D. T. Niles, a Methodist evangelist from Ceylon—now Sri Lanka—that seems to relate to this. There was a man in India, said Niles, who had been to a Billy Graham crusade and felt that he was saved during the meeting. Afterward, he was running home to tell his wife and family the good news when he stumbled across a blind beggar.

He paused in his flight long enough to make sure the man was all right. "I'm sorry," he said, "but I'm in a great hurry. You see, I have just found Christ at the Billy Graham meeting, and I am on my way home to tell my wife and family."

Niles paused for a moment, then quietly added: "He had just missed Christ where he might have found him—in the beggar."

There it is, isn't it? The conundrum. The mystery. What we think we see and what we don't. What we believe we know and what we fail to understand. It is very tantalizing. Reality shimmers like the surface of a pond when the wind blows on it. We think we see and we don't. We think we understand and we miss the point. He thought he was saved, but he missed Christ in the beggar.

Isn't this the point that Mark makes again and again in his Gospel? That it is God who is at work in Christ and if we don't see that then we don't see anything at all, everything we think we see is a mirage, an illusion? Jean-Paul Sartre said of Jean Genet, a dramatist who loved to create illusions, that he made us look at the whirligig. That's what Mark does, isn't it? He makes us look at the whirligig, and then we aren't sure what we're seeing, for it changes before our eyes.

Bartimaeus understood what the crowds of sighted folks around him didn't. He called to the man he couldn't see, "Jesus, Son of David, have mercy on me!"[3] Son of David was a messianic title. It meant that Bartimaeus was seeing to the heart of the mystery. He knew who Jesus really was. Beyond all the hub-

3. Mark 10:47.

bub, the celebrity status, the rumors, he understood: this was God's Messiah, the one who came as the edge of a new age that was dawning, of a totally revised creation! He was the very essence of what Mark was trying to say in his Gospel, that transcendence was breaking loose in our midst, and was doing so very specifically in the person of Jesus. Moreover, it was not something everybody could see or testify to. In good mystery style, it was vouchsafed to a blind man, to show that it wasn't something the philosophers or politicians or usual magi of the world would come to on their own. God alone was responsible for it, and only those prepared to abandon all their own devices for salvation could receive it.

In the tumult, Jesus stood still. He recognized the voice of a true seer when he heard it. "Call him here," he commanded. And they did. "Take heart," they said to Bartimaeus, the way worshipers are told "Lift up your hearts." "He is calling you."

"Throwing off his cloak," says the scripture, "he sprang up and came to Jesus."[4]

I picture it as if he were a flower suddenly bursting out of its green sheath and into blossom.

"What do you want me to do for you?" asked Jesus.[5]

Two men meeting in a timeless moment. One the Savior of the world. The other a blind man who knew the Savior of the world without seeing him. They belonged together, locked for a brief time in the intimacy of God's eternal will.

"Rabbi," said the blind man. "My teacher, let me see again."[6]

What did he mean, *again?* Had he been sighted before, like our friend who lost her sight as an adult? Or did he mean he wanted to see what he had seen a few moments before, Jesus as the Messiah, the Son of David, the anointed of God? Had the

4. Mark 10:50.
5. Mark 10:51.
6. Ibid.

vision waned, and was that what he desired most, to see it again, to be caught up in it as totally as before?

"Go," said Jesus, "your faith has made you well."[7]

Well—whole—complete as a person—saved—redeemed—renewed—himself in all his fullness.

And immediately—one of Mark's favorite words—*immediately!*—no waiting, no delay, instantly, with the speed of light—"he regained his sight and followed him (Jesus) on the way."[8]

What would you have done if, after years of darkness, you had suddenly received your sight? Surely there would have been people to run and tell, like the man who was saved at the Billy Graham meeting. There were many things you were waiting to see—sunsets, waterfalls, sparkling pools, tall buildings, leafy trees, starry skies, beds of flowers, birds and squirrels and dogs and cats.

Would you have followed Jesus on the way?

Yes. If you had seen what Bartimaeus saw, what that blind man saw. If you had seen the meaning of Jesus' presence, felt the impact of God's incarnation in a single man, understood that you were tremblingly in touch with the heart of all of redeemed reality. Then you too would have followed him on the way, for your heart would have gone after him the way a bit of metal follows a great magnet, an irresistible force, an overwhelming and undeniable power.

For what had happened to Bartimaeus—what happens to every true believer—was the radicalization of his life and vision. Everything about him had suddenly been transformed, raised to a new power, a new level of existence. It is hard to describe it, but that is what occurred. He was no longer the old Barti-

7. Mark 10:52.
8. Ibid.

maeus. He was a new man—whole, well, different. Everything about him was changed. He was Bartimaeus squared, radicalized, raised to the nth power.

Originally a blind man squatting by the road, helpless, powerless, without prospect, he was now what God wants every one of us to be, a son or daughter of the light, a child of forever, a person with total vision.

A question, perhaps two.

Don't you feel like a blind person huddled in darkness beside the road? And wouldn't you like to explode into fullness the way Bartimaeus did?

That is what Mark's Gospel is about. Nothing more, and nothing less.

The Abysmal Failure of
Earthly Religion

Mark 11:1-12:27

Brian Wren, the hymn writer, once told me about a church where an associate pastor remained on the staff through the tenures of seven senior ministers. The first, Rev. Smith, brought her to work with him. The second, Rev. Burke, was pleased to have her remain when he came, for he had heard wonderful things about her work with the young people. The third, a woman named Dewart-Jones, had known her in seminary and was delighted to be reunited with her. The fourth, Rev. Anstruther, was likewise happy to have her on staff during his tenure, as she had become a fixture and no senior minister dared remove her except at his peril. And so it went, through all seven pastors.

The only question, after this woman had served the church through the tenures of all seven ministers, was, "In the resurrection, whose associate minister will she be?"

Now that's a facetious story, but it is very similar to the one posed to Jesus in our text when a group of Pharisees and Herodians told about seven brothers who had all been married to the same woman, each without issue, and then asked, "In the resurrection whose wife will she be?"[1] They weren't being facetious. They merely thought they were being clever and that

1. Mark 12:23.

Jesus, the upstart rabbi, would be unable to answer the question to anybody's satisfaction.

He fooled them, of course. "When people rise from the dead," he said, "they neither marry nor are given in marriage, but are like angels in heaven."[2]

That is a hard text for all of us who have grown old thinking we shall be reunited with loved ones in heaven, isn't it? How about meeting with all those folks on the beautiful shore by and by? How many ministers have concluded funeral services for loved ones with the promise that we shall one day see those blessed faces again? And how many dear ones have we surrendered to death more easily because we have this indomitable hope that we shall rejoin them with hugs and kisses and joy when we ourselves cross over into the next life? What do Jesus' words to the Pharisees and Herodians do to that cherished idea of family reunions on the other side?

Lest any be too deeply disturbed by these questions, there are places in the scriptures where we are assured of such meetings with loved ones beyond death. Even the disciples' recognition of Jesus after his resurrection is part of such an assurance.

But it was not Mark's purpose to suggest or reinforce such a view in his Gospel. This response to the Pharisees and Herodians is characteristic of the gnostic viewpoint that governs the Gospel of Mark, which is that God is the Totality of all that is and those who die in him become a part of that totality. That is, they don't go to heaven to have a reunion with their families and sit around the campfire reminiscing about Aunt Susie and Cousin Thomas. They become spiritual beings like the angels, whose chief purpose is to dwell around the throne of the Almighty and join their praise with that of all the others.

2. Mark 12:25.

Look at the entire text—a long one!—we are dealing with.

First, there is the story of Jesus' entry into Jerusalem, the center of Jewish religion.[3] It is interesting, as scholars have long noted, that this is the first time Jesus was ever in the Holy City. In John's Gospel, the very opposite is true—he is often in Jerusalem, almost from the beginning. But Mark wanted us to understand one thing very clearly, that the real believers, the ones who understood what God was doing, were simple people in the countryside, not the sophisticated religious patrons in Jerusalem. In fact, as we'll see in other parts of the text, the sophisticated religious patrons were the ones who had got everything wrong!

Look at the next bit of narrative, the story of Jesus' cursing the fig tree.[4] The fig tree had long been a symbol of the nation of Israel. This wasn't merely a fig tree in the story, it was the nation of Israel itself. The tree had given every indication of bearing fruit, yet was totally barren of figs. So Jesus pronounced a curse on it, and when he and the disciples passed the same tree later that day the disciples noticed that it had shriveled and died. And even they must have made the connection.

Earlier that day, their master had thrown over the tables of the moneychangers in the temple and reproached the Jews for having turned the sacred space of God into something profitable for themselves. "My house shall be called a house of prayer for all the nations," he quoted from Isaiah 56:7, "but you have made it a den of robbers."[5]

I sometimes think of that image when I hear a preacher imploring people to give more money, don't you? Especially if I suspect that the money is not going to be used for any sacred purpose and the preacher is only hoping to enlarge either his

3. Mark 11:1-11.
4. Mark 11:12-24.
5. Mark 11:17.

reputation or his bank account.

The cursing of the fig tree must be regarded in light of this experience and the total disappointment of Jesus in the commercialization of the hallowed traditions of Judaism. What Jesus saw in Jerusalem was that Israel had failed as a spiritual entity. It had turned what God had given it into a system for the support of those in authority, without regard for the poor or anybody else. It did not deserve to live.

After the story of the fig tree in our text comes the parable Jesus told about the man who owned a vineyard and sent his servants to collect his due of the proceeds from the sale of grapes and wine. Each time he sent a servant, they beat him or killed him and threw him out of the vineyard. Finally, he sent his own son, thinking they must surely respect him. But they beat and killed him, as they had done to the others.[6]

It was a compelling story, set here as Jesus has so recently entered Jerusalem to bring his ministry to a climax. The shadow of the cross is already upon him and his disciples as they face the people controlling Israel's religious life. And anybody, except perhaps the scribes and Pharisees in charge of Jerusalem's spiritual welfare, can clearly see that Israel as a religious community is a failed experiment.

We cannot exult in this judgment against Israel, for the same judgment condemns our own religious institutions. One of the things we know about the growth and history of institutions is that they soon lose sight of the reasons that brought them into being and become so self-absorbed in their own success or failure that they cease to fulfill their original purposes. Every pastor has seen this in at least one old church he or she has pastored: an institution has grown far away from the real

6. Mark 12:1-11.

spiritual fervor that created it and now exists only to serve the whims and vanities of a group of trustees and deacons who enjoy having power and control. If Jesus were in a single night to whip through all the churches in Christendom, turning over tables and smashing things the way he did with the money-changers in the temple, the howl and stench from the churches would be noticed in every corner of the world.

Can we set a figure on it? Would this happen to sixty percent of all the churches now in existence? Seventy percent? Eighty percent? It is terrible to contemplate, isn't it?

Keith Miller, who became famous among evangelical Christians for his book *The Taste of New Wine*, wrote a later book called *The Dream*, which was surely inspired by Dickens' *A Christmas Carol*. In this little book, Miller, who is the narrator, is caught up by God one night and whisked around to church after church to see what is actually happening in them—how members vie for power, how they mistreat one another, how they fall unforgivably short of the ideals of love and grace.

In one church they visit, God or "The Presence," as Miller calls him, goes into the chancel as communion is being served and personally touches each communicant. It is a redemptive moment in an otherwise dull and uninspiring service. God afterwards tells him that he chose bread and wine for the elements in communion because they are part of everyone's life and it is easier to touch their souls when they are handling them.

Miller wants to know about churches that don't focus on communion as part of their worship.

"Well," says God slowly, "every church which is still around has *some* central channel in its worship service through which I can touch people's hearts. With some it's preaching—though it's tough, even for Me, to come through *some* of those sermons. And sometimes it's the music or the prayer or the reading of My Word. But if there is no definite, regular way for Me to meet each person in the worship service, that church just doesn't last long as one of Mine."

Miller is puzzled. What does God mean?

God explains:

> Such "churches" look like Christian churches on the outside. But if there's no place in their worship for regular living contact with Me, then they become psychological or sociological centers or historical societies in disguise—with an occasional nod to My Word or sacraments. If the ministers and people don't experience Me as being alive in their worship, then they have shut Me out of their community, whether they know it or not. And this sterile corporate plague has swept across several major denominations and evangelical groups in the past, leaving a spiritual wasteland which only has the faintest memory-trace of being a joyful outpost of My kingdom.[7]

How many churches that you know have a strong sense of God in them? How many are steeped in holiness and mystery? How many are filled with members who actually seem to be following Jesus?

I cannot count the times in a single year when I hear from ministers some awful tale of woe about how a congregation has

---

7. Keith Miller, *The Dream* (Word, 1985), pp. 39-40.

treated them or someone they care about. They invariably seem to be scandalized that Christians can behave so shamelessly toward others and yet pretend that they are following Jesus. One dear friend is presently so shattered by a recent experience with a congregation that he is undergoing therapy five days a week. He spends one hour on each of those days with a psychiatrist and two hours in group therapy. The reactions of others in his group therapy class are most telling: "How can people behave that way," they ask, "and continue to call themselves Christians?!"

Perhaps we never made the connection between these terrible stories about Israel's failure and our failure, or our collective failures and this apparently stand-alone story about the question of whose wife the woman would be in the life after the resurrection from the dead. But we can see it now, can't we? It isn't as isolated a narrative as we always assumed it was, for it too is a picture of our human shortsightedness, our failure to understand the nature of God's kingdom and the afterlife.

For isn't it just possible that most of our concepts of an afterlife are self-favoring? That we have conjured them up to comfort ourselves for the loss of loved ones who have died?

I admit I am guilty. I think more about death and the afterlife now that I am older. Sometimes I lie awake while my wife is sleeping by my side and think of how awful it would be to die, or for her to die, and for us not to be together any longer. Most of our lives have been spent together. I do not like to contemplate an afterlife in which we cannot continue to be together for eternity, even if there is an interval when one of us has gone and the other has not.

Yet I have to confess that this is a very selfish attitude. The idea of knowing our loved ones after death, and being in their company, has been carefully cultivated through the centuries. My friend George Docherty, who was Peter Marshall's successor at the New York Avenue Presbyterian Church in Washington, DC, told me once about visiting a lady parishioner in Aberdeen, Scotland, whose husband Sandy wanted nothing to do with religion. He had a beautiful garden, with flowers and fruit trees and grass as smooth as a billiard table, and said, "I dinna need to come to church; my garden is all the religion I need." A few months later, his wife sickened and died. George went to visit Sandy, and found his once-beautiful garden grown up in weeds. "Sandy," he asked, "what good is your garden now?" And he proceeded to witness to Sandy about faith and the afterlife, asking if he didn't want to see his wife again, and won him to Christ. I would probably have done the same thing if I had been in George's shoes. But was it honest? Isn't the very idea of continued relationship after death filled with human self-interest? Isn't it at least slightly less than *spiritual?*

If Mark's story about Jesus' answer to the Pharisees and Herodians is true, and Jesus did say to them that in heaven there will be no marriage or giving in marriage, for all will be like angels, then isn't it also true that the real aim of our entire existence is not to perpetuate the relationships we have here on earth but to become one with God, who is the Totality of everything, and to worship him and enhance his lordship throughout eternity?

The Gospel of Mark brooks no compromise on religious principles. Again and again, the disciples are taken to task for not seeing the spiritual truth of things, for being blinded by earthly appearances and failing to make the grade as insightful and knowledgeable followers. This story is merely another such moment in their long and difficult tutelage. They too must learn to understand what the Pharisees and Herodians didn't, that true spirituality is much higher and more ethereal than we presently regard it as being. It demands our total surrender of earthly values and our complete acceptance of a new level of being, a transcendent level, in which we are no longer plodding, earthly disciples but are like the very angels in heaven.

There is one more step in this fascinating text—a kind of epilogue to it—and that is Jesus' answer when the scribes asked him to name the greatest commandment. Jesus didn't hesitate to name it: "The first is, 'Hear, O Israel: the Lord our God, the Lord is one; you shall love the Lord your God with all your heart, and with all your soul, and with all your mind, and with all your strength.'"[8] What we have been saying about God as Pleroma and Totality is pertinent. God is *one*, and we are to love God, love the oneness, with everything in us and everything we are. We are to love and adore the Totality.

The second greatest commandment, says Jesus, is: "You shall love your neighbor as yourself."[9] That is, when we are in love with the Totality, we shall desire the neighbor's good as much as our own, for the neighbor too is part of the Totality.

One of the scribes agrees. Doing this, he says—adoring the Totality, both in God and in one's neighbor—"is more important than all whole burnt offerings and sacrifices."[10] He is a good man, for he sees the truth. What he has said encapsulates this entire text, reemphasizing all that it has said about the inadequacy of earthly religion.

No wonder Jesus says he is not far from the kingdom of God.

8. Mark 12:29-30.
9. Mark 12:31.
10. Mark 12:33.

Everybody Needs
a Little Apocalypse

Mark 13:1-36

The title of this sermon is intended to be only partly facetious. It is, to begin with, a play on the title scholars have long given to the thirteenth chapter of the Gospel of Mark, the Little Apocalypse. For some readers, it seems out of character with the rest of the Gospel, for the Jesus who speaks all the dire warnings of this chapter sounds uncommonly harsh and imperious compared with the healing and sympathy he exudes in other parts of the Gospel. But the chapter is also a reminder of the realities of the spiritual world—assuming that one believes the spiritual world is real. For, however much we would like to forget the fact, the war between good and evil is fierce and undying, and, according to both Jewish and Christian doctrine, a time will come when that contest becomes cataclysmic!

As I say, we aren't fond of remembering this. We'd much prefer to go blithely through our confectionary world, with all its snazzy cars, fast foods, jet travel, fantasy movies, and two hundred varieties of tasty, nourishing breakfast cereal, as though that were the whole story and we didn't need to worry about a crunch time when all of that goes up in smoke. But the Bible has a nasty habit of reminding us that that isn't all there is and that we should only hope when the end comes that we are convincingly on God's side and not on the side of sloth and evil.

I sometimes wonder, when I'm strolling through a beautiful shopping mall with fountains and waterfalls and trees growing toward the skylight, and with dozens of pleasure palaces down every avenue, what it would be like to be in such a spot when the end finally comes. I can imagine the weeping and wailing—two good biblical words, by the way—and the scrambling that would take place as people tried to get outside, only to discover, if they did, that the disaster is universal and there is no escape from it.

But, as I said, we don't want to think about such dark things.

Notice, if you will, that the disaster Jesus speaks of in our text begins with the temple, the center of so-called religious faith in his nation. It doesn't begin in a saloon or an opium parlor or a pool hall or a whore house—all places that preachers have railed against through the years—but at the very heart and center of religious practice.

That must mean something, mustn't it? Maybe that the cosmic disaster, the great judgment on the world, begins in the place that gives the most offense to God. Not these other places that society has deemed less than sanctified and above reproach. But where people say their prayers and sing their hymns and speak reverentially of their love for God. God must be most offended by the pretensions of the faithful, not the open sinning of the masses. The faithful, who screw up their faces to look pious and speak sanctimoniously of the Bible and what it means to live by its precepts, but have not really grown in faith and come to the point of knowing Jesus for who he really was and is.

Perhaps this is why we don't often hear sermons on the thirteenth chapter of Mark—because its stories and predictions hit close enough to home to cause us some perturbation, an uneasiness we can't quite comprehend or describe. The faithful wouldn't like the preacher to suggest that God is ever harder on the faithful than on the unfaithful. But in the mind of Jesus he is!

[margin annotation: alarm disquiet]

Why did Mark include this strange apocalyptic passage that seems so unlike the rest of his Gospel? Was it because he was a Gnostic and Gnostics often wrote about such strange things? The long Gnostic tractate "On the Origin of the World" includes this passage:

> Before the consummation [of the age], the whole place will shake with great thundering. Then the rulers will be sad. … The angels will mourn for their mankind, and the demons will weep over their seasons, and their mankind will wail and scream at their death. Then the age will begin, and they will be disturbed. Their kings will be intoxicated with the fiery sword, and they will wage war against one another, so that the earth is intoxicated with bloodshed. And the seas will be disturbed by those wars. Then the sun will become dark. And the moon will cause its light to cease. The stars of the sky will cancel their circuits.[1]

But of course it wasn't only the Gnostics who fabricated such horrendous pictures of the end of the world. The book of

---

1. *The Nag Hammadi Library in English*, p. 188.

Daniel in the Old Testament is filled with them, and there are pieces of them in the so-called intertestamental literature, as well as in the best example of all, the book of Revelation.

If Mark needed a reason for including the thirteenth chapter of his Gospel, it was probably as simple as this: He had a Gnostic's contempt for the history and society of worldly people, coupled with a strong sense of the Hebrew justice that depicted God as avenging the poor and downtrodden by overturning the world as we know it. For him, the dark sayings of Jesus in this chapter are a flaming challenge to the status quo, to a careless world order in which people pay little attention to true holiness and transcendence.

If any verification of such a theory is needed, it may exist in the few verses that precede the chapter, Mark 12:41-44, which tell the story of the poor widow Jesus observes casting her two small coins into the temple treasury. "Truly I tell you," says Jesus to the disciples, "this poor widow has put in more than all those who are contributing to the treasury. For all of them have contributed out of their abundance; but she out of her poverty has put in everything she had, all she had to live on." There is the kind of rank injustice or unevenness of devotion that would cause God to bring all things to an end, for God does not look on the size of the gifts of the faithful but on the intent of their hearts, and most contributors only made their offerings because they wished to be seen for their munificence.

Back to the title of the sermon.

Apocalyptic isn't only for groups and nations, is it? We all need a little of it in our daily lives. We need it to remind us that life and prosperity aren't forever in this world. There is always a time of reckoning coming toward us. Jesus' message "Keep alert"[2] is intended for us as surely as it was for the disciples. We are part of the household of slaves who have been left to do their duties while the Master is traveling, and do not know when he will return to call us to account.

As a pastor, I have often seen parishioners who were totally surprised by a sudden illness, an incapacitating injury, or the tragic loss of a family member, and have heard their protestations of unpreparedness. "Oh, if I had only been more careful," said one. "I wasn't ready for this," said another, "and now I can never fulfill my obligations." "I should have known," said yet another, "God cannot be pleased with my slovenliness."

Once, I buried a young man—barely forty years old—who was an entrepreneur and an avid runner. He was tall, well built, and apparently in excellent physical shape. He ran four or five miles every morning before going to his office, where he made some enviable deals and a lot of money. One morning his heart exploded half-way through his run. Nobody was near him when it happened, but a motorist saw him lying beside the road and called 911. His body was still warm when the medics arrived, but there was nothing they could do for him. His time had come—unexpectedly.

I visited several times with his widow. The first time she was in deep shock and distress over the loss of her husband. The fifth or sixth time, she was in equally deep shock over the shape his affairs were in. He had been reckless in the market, and owed a lot of money. They had four children, the oldest of whom was twelve. "How am I going to educate these children?" she asked forlornly. Then she told me she would have to give up the lovely house where they lived and move to something a

2. Mark 13:33.

lot less expensive. Her husband had not been ready to die. He hadn't expected to. I could only hope his soul was in better shape than his estate.

The same could be said for most of us, that we simply aren't prepared for any kind of judgment, either fiscal or spiritual. And Jesus, whose concern was always for the spiritual, sounded a clear warning sound. Things aren't always going to rock along the way they are now.

So be ready!

No Greater Love

Mark 14:1-31

Mark didn't have to be a Gnostic to see the extent to which the unnamed woman in this passage loved Jesus. But being a Gnostic didn't hurt, for Gnostics were a lot more conscious of the spiritual importance of women than almost anybody else in their time. Many of them worshiped under Gnostic priestesses. It may have chafed them that there wasn't a single woman listed among Jesus' twelve disciples, the ones who inherited his mantle in the early church. But the Gospel of Mark tried to make restitution. There were several important women in its brief narratives: the woman with an issue of blood[1]; the young girl, daughter of a synagogue leader, whom Jesus raised from the dead[2]; the Syrophoenician woman with a sick daughter[3]; the poor widow who gave all she had to the temple treasury[4]; this nameless woman who anointed Jesus' feet[5]; the two Marys who were among those watching at the cross[6]; and, finally, the same two women, plus Salome, who came to Jesus' tomb and learned that he wasn't there.[7]

We know more about the Gnostics' regard for women from reading the Gospel of Mary, one of the tractates recovered in

1. Mark 5:24-34.
2. Mark 5:21-24, 35-43.
3. Mark 7:24-30.
4. Mark 12:41-46.
5. Mark 14:3-9.
6. Mark 15:40-41.
7. Mark 16:1-8.

the Nag Hammadi Library. According to this beautiful little fragment, the disciples were worried after Jesus commanded them to preach the Gospel everywhere. "How shall we go to the gentiles and preach the gospel of the kingdom of the Son of Man?" they asked, weeping. "If they did not spare him, how will they spare us?"

It was not one of the men who comforted them and charged them to fulfill their duty, but Mary Magdalene. "Do not weep and do not grieve nor be irresolute," she counseled them, "for his grace will be entirely with you and will protect you. But rather let us praise his greatness, for he has prepared us and made us into men."[8]

At this, Peter said to Mary, "Sister, we know that the Savior loved you more than the rest of women. Tell us the words of the Savior which you remember—which you know (but) we do not, nor have we heard them."[9] She then disclosed to them a vision she had had of the Lord, and told them what he had said to her.

Some scholars think that this nameless woman in our text was Mary Magdalene, the one Jesus loved "more than the rest of women." Others side with the Gospel of John, which sets the occasion in the home of Mary, Martha, and Lazarus, Jesus' friends in Bethany, and depicts that Mary as performing this oblation.[10]

Personally, I prefer to think it was Mary Magdalene, whom Mark mentioned again after Jesus' death, while he didn't ever refer to the Mary in Bethany. Also, Mark says the event occurred in the home of Simon the Leper, while John says it happened in the home of Lazarus. I believe John changed the details of his narrative to make a connection with his story of

8. *The Nag Hammadi Library in English*, p. 525.
9. Ibid.
10. John 12:1-8.

the raising of Lazarus, which was positioned shortly before this story and involved a long discussion between Jesus and the Mary who was Lazarus' sister.

Regardless of which Mary it was, though, the act was one of enormous personal sacrifice, for both Mark and John refer to the complaint that the perfume or ointment was valued at more than 300 denarii, the amount an ordinary worker could earn in an entire year. Ointments were not uncommon. Compounded of an olive oil base with various aromatic spices added to it, they were kept in vials or flasks, often made of alabaster, and used in moderation to anoint the heads of visiting friends or loved ones and thus surround them with a pleasant aroma. In Egypt, they were also employed to embalm the dead, and many commentators see Mary's act as a prefiguring of Jesus' death and entombment. Mark, in fact, has Jesus identifying it as such a symbol of his burial. Whatever its meaning, though, the important thing here is the cost of the ointment: Mary clearly adored Jesus and thought he was worth the expenditure!

What is the insight Mark intends by including this action? What indeed but the underlining of the utter totality with which Jesus' followers should regard him. The Gospel of John makes the same point by having Judas Iscariot, who was already conspiring with the high priests against Jesus, be the one who complained about how valuable the ointment was. Of course Judas, who was Mary's diametrical opposite, would not understand such devotional extravagance.

For Mark, this self-forgetful adoration was what was required of anyone who really knew Jesus—knew him in the Gnostic sense of realizing who he was, that he was God's anointed one, God manifest in human form. Being a woman, Mary didn't "know" as much as the scribes and Pharisees. She may not have known as much as the disciples, who had been with Jesus more often when he was healing or teaching. But she knew something with her inner mind and heart, and Jesus was everything to her. Even if the ointment had been purchased for her own embalming after she was dead, it no longer mattered. Her own death no longer mattered. Jesus was all that mattered, now and forever.

We seldom witness such devotion.

I heard about it once from a friend named Sasha Makovkin. Sasha creates beautiful pottery in the wooded hills above Mendocino, California. His father came to this country from Russia. His uncle, his father's brother, was a priest in Moscow. During the Russian revolution, the Cossacks entered the uncle's church and carried all the icons and crosses into the square outside. Then they marched the uncle outside at gunpoint. They told him that if he would walk across the square, treading on the icons and crosses, they would release him. He refused and was shot and killed.

There have been many such martyrs in the history of the faith. Most of them were like Mary. They knew who Jesus was and what they knew consumed them, demanded that they behave profligately with their own lives and possessions in order to honor him.

But most of Jesus' followers didn't understand this. They were still debating within themselves whether to follow him at any price. The same is true of many of his followers today. We stop to ask, "Is this stand worth it? Do I really want to give up everything for Jesus?"

If we have to ask, we have not yet grasped what Mary knew. And it has not yet grasped us.

May I make a confession? I was tempted to conclude this sermon at this point, but felt that it needed something more. I wanted a really knockout story about someone who had given up everything for Jesus, so I riffled through my notebooks in search of one. There were two contenders. One was in a note I made years ago in Winchester Cathedral in England. Near the Lady Chapel in that beautiful church is a pedestal and brass figure of William Walker, a diver, who "saved the cathedral with his own hands" by replacing the rotten underpinnings of the building when there were no funds to do so.

The other story alluded to an article in the *Christian Century* for August 18, 1981, about a *Century* correspondent named Gerald Forshey and his family, who elected, during the so-called white flight from certain parts of Chicago, to remain where they were, in a rapidly changing neighborhood, as a witness to their faith in Christ and love for Christ's little ones. One night they came home and found their house burglarized and desecrated, with sofas ripped apart, picture frames destroyed, and excrement smeared on the walls. The next morning they held a family council to review their situation. They prayed a long time and then voted to stay where they were, unwilling to give up on Jesus and the love they had vowed to have for others.

But somehow these didn't seem to be the right touches for the ending of this sermon. As I lay awake before dawn thinking about it, I felt an impulse to go on with Mary's story itself, trying to imagine what it must have been like for her to anoint Jesus' head with her costly perfume. If she had used only a little—the customary dab—I'm sure nothing would have been said about it. But she was compelled to anoint Jesus with *all* of it, as if it wouldn't be enough—it wouldn't *say* enough—if she used only a little.

It was clear, in other words, that she felt *passionately* about what she was doing. So what was going on in her mind to make her feel the way she did?

Perhaps, with a woman's uncanny prescience, she knew Jesus didn't have much longer to be with his followers. She discerned, even more than the disciples, that his enemies were closing in and the end was near. She may even have seen it in his eyes, felt it in his bearing, for he surely knew the confrontation was upon him.

And she owed him so much. Luke, in his Gospel,[11] says Jesus cast seven demons out of her, indicating that she had been either very ill, very troubled, or, as rumor came to have it, very promiscuous. In any event, she appears to have been so transformed by her redemption that she naturally became the leader of a band of women who followed Jesus much as the disciples did, as she was always named first among them.

Given this combination, of prescience and passion, she must have felt totally compelled to anoint Jesus as she did. She might have begun with the intention of using only a small amount of the ointment, as she might have done with the others who were present. But when she came to Jesus she was so overpowered by her emotions—by her great love for him and her dread of what might be about to befall him—that she could not resist the impulse simply to pour all the ointment into his hair, bespeaking her passionate love for him and foreshadowing the death he was about to die.

11. Luke 8:2.

Frankly, I am captivated by this image. Or not the image so much as the emotion it signifies—an overwhelming, irresistible tide of emotion that could not be brooked by any sense of reason or reserve. She *had* to do it! There was no way around it. She would have burst if she hadn't done it, and would have lived with regret ever after. What fascinates me and will not let me go is the split second when she knew she had to do it and immediately did what she felt compelled to do.

I wonder how many of us have such split seconds from time to time without acting on them, without following through and doing what we momentarily want to do. We temporize—that's the word, isn't it?—we put off the impulse just long enough to get the better of it and let it die unfulfilled. We save ourselves from the difficult or expensive or hare-brained thing we were about to commit to by staving it off just long enough to stifle and elude it.

And that is our downfall as followers of Jesus.

How often do we miss the opportunity of becoming all that God wants us to be by this brief act of resistance and delay? How many of us have failed to become Jesus' followers— turned away from some special calling or extraordinary commitment—because we didn't follow through on a magnificent impulse like Mary's?

Jesus said of Mary's act, "Wherever the good news is proclaimed in the whole world, what she has done will be told in remembrance of her."[12] It's true, isn't it? We are talking about it now because of its extraordinariness, its amazing prodigality and generosity.

Maybe this was the note I knew was missing from the sermon. The reminder to all of us that those split seconds like the

12. Mark 14:9.

one in which Mary did this extravagant thing are in the end the ones that determine our destiny. They offer us, however briefly, what the poet called the road "less traveled by."[13] Whatever invitation they hold—to follow a calling, to make a stupendous gift, to rescue a drowning person, to save a worthy institution, to reach out to an enemy—they are the momentary paths to salvation.

I think Mark would have concurred. They are the way into the kingdom of God.

13. Robert Frost, "The Road Not Taken," in *Robert Frost's Poems* (Washington Square Press, 1977), p. 223.

In the Company of Deserters

Mark 14:22-31

In Pär Lagerkvist's *Barabbas*, his novel about the man who was released when Jesus was crucified, there is a poignant scene in which Barabbas is challenged about his new-found faith in the one who died in his place. He is working as a slave in a copper mine on the island of Cyprus, and, like the other slaves, wears a chain with a disk declaring him to be the property of the Roman government.

A fellow slave, an old Armenian named Sahak, has had an extra inscription inscribed on the back of his disk. It is the name of his Savior, *Christos Iesus*. He shows it to Barabbas and lets him hold it and run his finger over it. It means, he says, that he really belongs to the Son of God, not to the Romans.

Barabbas is impressed, and wants the same carving on the back of his disk. Working slowly and secretly, Sahak scratches identical marks on the rear side of Barabbas' disk. He is still a slave, but now he too belongs to the Galilean.

But someone has overheard about the carvings. He tells a guard and the guard passes the word along. Eventually it reaches the governor. The governor has Sahak and Barabbas brought before him. He examines the carvings and then offers them their lives if they will repudiate the god whose name is on the back of their disks.

Sahak refuses.

The governor asks Barabbas if he wants to die for the god whose name is on his disk.

Barabbas stands silent. At last he mumbles, "I have no god."

The governor asks why he has the name on his disk, then.

"Because I want to believe," says Barabbas.

The governor offers Sahak a final chance to renounce the one whose name adorns his disk. Sahak is resolute. The governor orders the guard to take him out and execute him.

While the guard is coming, he takes his knife and crosses out the name of Jesus on the back of Barabbas's disk.[1]

For the rest of his troubled life, wherever he goes and whatever he does, Barabbas must bear that crossed-out name on his disk.

It is a sad, sad business.

I cannot say how many times through the years I had read our passage of scripture—for the last twenty years at least in the New Revised Standard Version—and I could not remember having ever noticed the power of those five words spoken by Jesus after he shared the bread and the cup with his followers: "You will all be deserters."

Imagine how they must have struck the disciples!

They had been with Jesus—how long, two or three years? They had started with him in Capernaum, on the Sea of Galilee. They had gone up to the mountains with him. They had traveled all the way to Jerusalem with him—on foot! They had watched him perform miracles of healing. They had heard his unforgettable sayings. Now they were eating a final meal with him, when they all knew the trouble he was in, with the authorities closing in like some great vice preparing to squeeze

1. Pär Lagerkvist, *Barabbas* (Random House, 1951), pp. 143-144.

the life out of him. It was a high moment, a sacred moment. And then he spoiled it!

"You will all be deserters."[2]

Wow! Double wow!

They would all wear the crossed-out name of Jesus.

It *is* a sad business, isn't it? For we all wear that stigma in one way or another. Some of us failed to stand up for him when we had a chance; it simply wouldn't have been popular. Others of us did things of which we were ashamed, and knew they were marks against him; they would have made him ashamed of us. And others of us—perhaps the greatest number—simply drifted away from him. We once professed our love, the way the disciples did. We enrolled. We joined the church, we attended Sunday school and Youth Group and whatever else was an applicable part of the church's program. But then we lost interest. We became disenchanted with the pastor or the music director. Somebody made us angry. We didn't feel welcome any more. We found other things to do. We went whole days without thinking of Jesus. Then weeks. Then months, and maybe years.

I have even had ministers admit as much to me. They began their journeys with high hopes and strong resolution. But the sun was hot and the way was hard. Their churches became burdensome. One day became pretty much like the one before. They felt stuck, as if they weren't going anywhere or getting anything accomplished. They began to wonder if they hadn't made a bad choice. They still talked about Jesus on Sunday, but only because it was expected, not because they were excited.

I said it is sad.

That crossed-out name. On all of us.

2. Mark 14:27.

"You will all be deserters."

Wouldn't it have been kind of Mark to omit this? He made editorial choices as he wrote his book. He doubtless left out other things. Why not this five-word statement by Jesus? Did it have to be included? It seems so—negative.

Maybe Mark had two reasons for including it.

First, there is a sense in which it is encouraging. For if all the apostles deserted him, yet returned and served the early church with bravery and distinction, then there is a chance for all deserters, isn't there? Even some of us who have ignored him for years. There's still an opportunity to come back, to serve, to be redeemed.

And, second, it serves Mark's purpose, the one he has been at pains to exhibit all the way through his Gospel, of saying what dunces the disciples were and how slow they were to come to an understanding of who Jesus was and what they had to do to enter the kingdom of God. After the two wilderness feedings, they still didn't understand, and quibbled over not having brought any bread with them. Even after the transfiguration before Peter, James, and John, James and John would come to him and ask to sit at his right and left hand in his kingdom, as if it were an ordinary kingdom and he could grant them such a favor.

Nor could they get it through their heads that the Son of Man, the Savior of the world, should suffer and die on a cross. That was the most humiliating and embarrassing part of all—the public exposure, everybody's jeering and shouting for him to be crucified. What was God thinking, if he was indeed the one sent from God?!

They *cared* about the flesh and humiliation. That was the

point. They still hadn't seen through the veil to the truth, that death is nothing, that a man can have power over his own death if only he knows the truth and is faithful to it.

Gnostics—those who were given to know and believe—despised the flesh and all the vicissitudes to which it is prone. Their loyalty was to something higher, the spirit, the *soul*. They saw through the cross and the mundanity of a death. They looked beyond it. They knew that the Lord who had healed the lame and the sick, who had fed multitudes in the wilderness, and who was recognized by the blind, the people with no *physical* sight, was immune to death.

None of this is easy to learn, is it? Like the disciples, we too care about flesh and humiliation. We care about most material things—staying well, having plenty of money, living in big houses, and driving powerful cars. Listen to the spiel of most of the TV evangelists about asking God for the things we want. Imagine that, the things *we* want! Computers, boats, video games, giant TV screens, vintage wines, expensive dinners, jet travel, trips to the Caribbean.

What do these things have to do with spirituality, with the kingdom of God? They *deflect* us from the kingdom, don't they? They don't really show us the way into it. Anybody who becomes a follower of Jesus in order to receive these things *starts out* with the crossed-out name of Jesus on his or her disk, doesn't he—or she? That isn't real Christianity at all. Or, if it is, Christianity is not about Jesus any more, it's about a materially-oriented religion that misses the mark completely.

Okay. This is where we are. We have all betrayed him. Some of us many times. Some of us for years. So what do we do now? How do we get back on track?

If we want to, that is.

That may be the key, right there. *If we want to.*

What made the disciples want to? They obviously came back. They rallied around after the crucifixion. They became pillars of the church. Some of them even gave their lives for their faith.

Why?

Because Jesus survived death.

We don't understand it. They didn't understand it. It was a mystery. Perhaps John's Gospel plumbs it more than the others. He shows the little band of disciples back in the upper room where they'd eaten that final meal with him—the place of their accusation—and with the door locked. They were afraid and they were hiding out. And suddenly, as the Gospel puts it so simply, "Jesus came and stood among them and said, 'Peace be with you.'"[3] *Shalom aleichem.* The common greeting among Jews, equivalent to "Hello."

Thomas, who was absent from that meeting, said he would not believe it was the Master unless he could see the imprints of the nails in his hands and the knife wound in his side. And a week later, when they were gathered in the same place, Thomas was there when Jesus appeared again.

"*Shalom aleichem,*" he said. And he invited Thomas to feel the nail prints and the riven place in his side.

But Thomas didn't need to do that. "My Lord and my God!" he exclaimed.[4]

Apparently this was what it took to get through to the thickheaded disciples. Finally they understood.

But we can't blame them. We too have a hard time believing such things. If only we could see what they saw, feel what they

3. John 20:19.
4. John 20:28.

felt, hear what they heard.

This is why Jesus said, after Thomas' outburst of faith, "Have you believed because you have seen me? Blessed are those who have not seen and yet have come to believe."[5]

Does this mean we don't have a snowball's chance in you-know-where of believing in Jesus because we haven't seen what they saw? No. Jesus himself said some would believe without seeing. And there had been a few all along the way—even a blind man—who knew without seeing the outcome of it all.

The important thing is to keep looking, keep believing, and not give up because we haven't had a life-changing experience—and our lives will be changed in the process.

When I was a pastor in Los Angeles, I met an extraordinarily personable man named Art Hutton. Art ran a Christian camp. The more I talked to him, the more mystified I became that a man of his extraordinary gifts and knowledgeability should be managing a camp.

When I expressed this to him, he laughed and told me his story.

He had been the manager of the Convention Center in Las Vegas—one of the busiest, most demanding jobs in the world. He was also a Christian, and said he had been finding himself drawn more and more to the church and less and less to the kind of big business he dealt with during the week. He accepted a job as elder in his church, and then a job as scoutmaster for the church's scout troupe. But something was gnawing at him, he said, asking for more.

One Sunday morning, his pastor preached a particularly moving sermon. It was a challenge to renewed discipleship. That night, still thinking about it, Art went out into his back-

5. John 20:29.

yard in the moonlight and asked God to show him what he could do to have a more fulfilling life as a follower of Jesus.

A couple of days later, one of his children returned from spending a few days at Cedar Crest Christian Camp near Oakhurst, California, and said, "Dad, I've found a job for you."

"Oh?" said Art. "And what might that be?"

"They need a new manager at Cedar Crest."

"I couldn't believe it," Art told me. "I had just asked God to show me what to do, and here was my child coming home with the answer."

Art didn't waste any time. Within two weeks, he had applied for the job at the camp and got it. He said his mother was astounded that he would take a job that paid only a small fraction of what he had been earning at the Convention Center.

"But I'm happier than I've ever been in my life," he told me, "because I'm doing exactly what I think God wants me to do."

I don't know if Art is still in that job or if he has had the kind of insight into the kingdom of God that Mark attributed to a few special people in his Gospel—the paralytic who was healed, the blind man Bartimaeus, Mary who anointed Jesus' head with expensive ointment—but I firmly believe he was in line for such an insight. He was doing what he believed God wanted him to do with his life, regardless of the material loss it caused him, and he was happy doing it.

It couldn't have been far from where he was to the kingdom of God.

The Matter of the Body

Mark 14:32-15:47

The human body, as all of us eventually discover, can be a very frail affair. As wonderful as it is, it has many limitations. Even if it survives childhood and early adulthood, sooner or later it starts to flag. A vein clogs up here, a joint seizes up there, and one day it all shuts down. No matter how much money we have or how famous we have become, we cannot indefinitely stave off the end, for death is unavoidable. As someone has said, the death rate is still what it always was: one per person!

One of the remarkable things about this section of the Gospel of Mark is its thematic focus on the body of Jesus. Most of the Gospel is about his transcendent spirit, which was God Manifest to the world. But in this part, it shines its light on his body and what happens to it in the space of a very few hours.

First, we see his body at prayer. He takes his disciples to Gethsemane, an olive orchard on the outskirts of Jerusalem, charges them with staying awake, and, going a little further, *throws himself* on the ground and prays that, if possible, God will save him from the bitter cup he realizes he is about to drink. The disciples don't stay awake, of course; they are as sluggish in body as they have proven in mind. The first time he returns and finds them asleep, he rouses Peter and says, "Simon, are you asleep? Could you not keep awake one hour? Keep awake and pray that you may not come into the time of trial; the spirit indeed is willing, but the flesh is weak."[1]

The spirit is *prothumon*, says Jesus—not just "willing," but "eager" and "cheerful"—"ready to spring up"! While the flesh is *dothenes*—"yielding" and "giving way."

One is a thoroughbred eager to burst out of the gate. The other is an old nag ready for the glue factory, weak and sagging and looking forward to death.

This is a familiar theme in Gnosticism: the spirit is infinitely superior to the flesh. It was not a new idea. Plato had taught it centuries before Christ, and most of the mystery cults took it up. The Gnostics in the early Christian movement universally believed in the triumph of mind or spirit over the body.

Elaine Pagels, in *The Gnostic Gospels*, assembles various Gnostic texts which reveal a widespread belief that, while Jesus' body may have actually suffered on the cross, he himself (i.e., his spirit) transcended the experience. She cites, for example, *The Apocalypse of Peter*, part of the Nag Hammadi Library, in which Peter speaks of seeing an ethereal figure above the cross that was "glad and laughing" while the nails were driven into Jesus' hands and feet. The Savior said to him, Peter reported, "He whom you saw being glad and laughing above the cross is the Living Jesus. But he into whose hands and feet they are driving the nails is his fleshly part, which is the substitute. They put to shame that which remained in his likeness. And look at him, and [look at] me!"[2]

---

1. Mark 14:37-38.

2. Apocalypse of Peter, 81:4-24, in *The Nag Hammadi Library in English*, p. 344; cited in Elaine Pagels, *The Gnostic Gospels* (Vintage Books, 1989), p. 72. Pagels also quotes *The Acts of John*, a famous Gnostic text discovered before Nag Hammadi, which reports that Jesus was more transcendent than physical and assumed various physical appearances. One time when John meant to touch Jesus, he said, "I encountered a material, solid body; but at other times again when I felt him, his substance

The idea that Jesus was not fully human was of course eventually condemned by the church councils and was part of the basis for declaring Gnosticism a heresy. But the Gospel of Mark, whether it represents full blown Gnosticism or not, appears in our text to have treated the physical body as if it were in all respects inferior to the mind or spirit of Jesus.

Consider the rapidly developing acts of this little drama:

First, there is the capture of Jesus and the farce of a trial with its conflicting witnesses.[3] Jesus himself remains aloof through the proceedings, deigning to speak only at the end, when the high priest asks him point blank if he is the Messiah. "I am," he says—*Ego eimi*, the words uttered by God when Moses asked his name—"and you will see the Son of Man seated at the right hand of the Power, and coming with the clouds of heaven."[4] There is a kind of august, untouchable spirit in these words, a promise of coming enthronement and retribution.

Then there is the angry reaction of the high priest and the condemnation of the entire council, who spit on him, blindfold him, and derisively cry "Prophesy!" to him, followed by the brief report, "The guards also took him over and beat him."[5]

When daylight comes, the chief priests consult with the elders and scribes and entire council, then bind Jesus and have him taken to Pilate, the Roman procurator.[6] Condemned by the religious authorities, he is now to answer to secular authority, as it alone has the power to crucify wrongdoers. Once again, Jesus remains stoical and imperiously silent, so that Pilate is amazed and apparently feels sympathy for him. But when Pilate tries to release him under the government's custom of freeing

was immaterial and incorporeal ... as if it did not exist at all." (*Acts of John*, in Edgar Hennecke, *New Testament Apocrypha* II [Philadelphia: Westminster Press], pp. 188-258; cited in Pagels, op. cit., p. 73).

3. Mark 14:53-59.
4. Mark 14:62.
5. Mark 14:65.
6. Mark 15:1.

a prisoner on the eve of Passover, the priests whip up the crowds to demand the release of Barabbas instead of Jesus, whom they now satirize as "King of the Jews," and Jesus is turned over to the soldiers to be crucified.[7]

The soldiers lead him out into the courtyard of the governor's palace, where he is covered with a purple robe (for mock royalty) and physically subjected to abuse and humiliation by the entire cohort of soldiers. Then he is taken to Golgotha, the place of crucifixion.[8] A passerby named Simon is conscripted to carry his cross, suggesting that by this time he has been beaten so severely that he is unable to do it himself. Yet when he is offered the customary mixture of wine and myrrh, employed as an anodyne for pain, he refuses it, as if he remains aloof to all proceedings having to do with his body.[9]

The derision of course continues when he is crucified. Miscellaneous voices taunt him about being unable to save himself. Even the bandits being crucified with him join in the ritual of humiliation.[10] At noon, there is a sudden, inexplicable darkness over the earth, and at three Jesus cries with a loud voice, saying "My God, my God, why have you forsaken me?" Then he gives another loud cry and breathes his last. And at this moment the curtain of the temple, a finely woven cloth dividing the outer court from the Holy of Holies, is rent from top to bottom.[11]

The centurion who stands near Jesus as he dies exclaims (according to Mark), "Truly this man was God's Son!"[12] Apparently this is afterward reported to the followers of Jesus by Mary Magdalene and some other women who came up with

---

7. Mark 15:6-15.

8. Mark 15:16-20.

9. Mark 15:21-24.

10. Mark 15:32; Mark does not report the story in Luke 23:39-42 about the bandit who asked Jesus to remember him in Paradise.

11. Mark 15:33-38.

12. Mark 15:39.

him to Jerusalem and are viewing everything from a distance.[13]

The final act for Jesus' body is for it to be removed from the cross and placed in a tomb belonging to a member of the Sanhedrin named Joseph of Arimathea, who boldly goes to Pilate and requests superintendency of the body, then takes it down, wraps it in a linen cloth, and has it transported to its resting place. Once more, Mary Magdalene (accompanied by Mary, the mother of Joses) follows and sees where the body is laid.[14]

Note the way Jesus remains transcendent in all of this drama involving his body. His quiet demeanor could be interpreted as mere stoicism, an inner discipline against expressing pain and discomfort of any kind, similar to that described in the cases of unusually heroic persons under torture. Or, read through the template of the Gnostics, it could be seen as a dismissal of the flesh as basically unimportant in the final scheme of things, and, even if Jesus actually suffered from torture and crucifixion, his obvious spiritual superiority to the woes of corporeal existence.

It is perhaps part of the artistry of Mark that our judgment about this can be swayed in either direction depending on our presuppositions and how we wish the matter to be resolved. But even if Mark was not Gnostic and was not attempting to sway us toward a particular interpretation of the facts, it must be observed that he dealt with all these admittedly dramatic happenings in the final hours of Jesus' life with an incredible swiftness and matter-of-factness, as if they were not really as important as many of the stories already narrated in his Gospel—say, the healing of the paralytic,[15] the quelling of the storms,[16] the healing of the Gerasene demoniac and the woman

13. Mark 15:40-41.
14. Mark 15:42-47.
15. Mark 2:1-12.
16. Mark 4:35-41, 6:45-52.

with an issue of blood,[17] the raising of the dead maiden,[18] the two feeding miracles,[19] and the encounter with blind Bartimaeus.[20]

Either way, then, Gnostic or not, the Gospel is instructive in this text about how, as followers of Jesus, we might come to think about our own bodies and the various ailments and frailties to which we are prone. Our physical sufferings, while they ought never to be minimized or ridiculed, are nevertheless bearable if we are able to hold them in perspective. That is, if we can regard them as temporary and in any way usable for the instruction and disciplining of our spirits.

As a pastor, I have been privileged to know many wonderful saints who bore their afflictions with incredible patience and fortitude—a woman whose cancer had spread through her body, so that she was often wracked by pain, but continued to pray for others as if that was the mission for which God was permitting her to stay alive; a woman who, though totally blind, sang in a gospel choir and braved the streets and subway system of New York City as if she were sighted; a paraplegic who came to church regularly and laughed aloud at the preacher's jokes; a teacher with Parkinson's disease who continued to stumble his way across campus and met his classes until a short time before his death; a young boy in braces who gave his crutches names and always had a smile on his face; and a middle-aged man whose cranial surgery left him with constant ringing in his ears but taught himself to think of it as a summons to meditation and the transformation of his life.

The Apostle Paul apparently shared Mark's viewpoint. "I consider that the sufferings of this present time," he wrote, "are not worth comparing with the glory about to be revealed to us,"

17. Mark 5:1-34.
18. Mark 5:35-43.
19. Mark 6:30-44, 8:1-10.
20. Mark 10:46-52.

because "all things work together for good for those who love God, who are called according to his purpose."[21] "Who will separate us from the love of Christ?" he asked.

> Will hardship, or distress, or persecution, or famine, or nakedness, or peril, or sword? As it is written, "For your sake we are being killed all day long; we are accounted as sheep to be slaughtered." No, in all these things we are more than conquerors through him who loved us. For I am convinced that neither death, nor life, nor angels, nor rulers, nor things present, nor things to come, nor powers, nor height, nor depth, nor anything else in all creation, will be able to separate us from the love of God in Christ Jesus our Lord.[22]

I remember the woman as if it were yesterday. She worked in the university where I taught, and in her mid-thirties was unmarried because she had stayed home to tend a sick mother, and, when her mother died, had inherited an ailing father in her place. She always appeared to be tired, and looked as if she hadn't had enough time to do her hair and apply her make-up, as both were done poorly. I think she came to talk from time to time because she was simply lonely and needed someone in whom to confide.

When her father died, she told me the story of his death. He had been smoking in bed—the one pleasure he still had, she said, as food tended to upset his stomach—and sometime in the night had set fire to his pajamas and bedclothes. She was sleeping next door and, smelling the smoke, leapt up and ran to her dad's room. Thinking quickly, she rolled him in the blan-

21. Romans 8:1, 28.
22. Romans 8:35-39.

ket, smothering the flames.

He pled with her not to send him to the hospital, for he knew he hadn't long to live and wanted to die at home. So she called his doctor to their home and the doctor tended his burns as well as he could and gave him some pills for the pain. He lingered for three days and died early one morning.

"I was awakened by his voice," she said, "and I got up immediately and rushed into his room, thinking he was calling me. But he was sitting up in bed, singing 'Amazing Grace.' He wasn't wearing a pajama top because his flesh was badly burned and he couldn't stand the clothing against his back. He was raising his arms in praise, and pieces of burned flesh were falling off as he reached out to God. Then he stopped singing and was gone. It was over very quickly. I straightened him in the bed and covered him with the sheet."

She was comforted by the way he died, and said she hoped that when her time came she would go as peaceably as he did.

There it is, isn't it, the flesh/spirit dilemma. And, in the end, we all know that it is the spirit that is most important.

The Hidden Easter

Mark 16:1-8

There is something I must share with you about the title and introduction of this sermon. As a preacher, I have always kept little notebooks in which to jot down unusual texts, sermon ideas, apt quotations, and stories I can use to illustrate my points. Even in retirement, I have continued the practice, for I still preach from time to time and need my notebooks. As I was going through them while writing an earlier sermon, I ran across this title, "The Hidden Easter," together with the textual note of Mark 16:1-8 and the following entry:

> Early memories of finding Easter eggs—always found them in clumps of tall, new grass—signs of life after winter's freezing temps. Is Easter *always* hidden? Hard to see the real transformations in the world. But God is at work!

At the time—the entry was made several years ago—I had not yet discovered the textual patterns in the Gospel of Mark that led to my writing *Hidden Mark*, and of course had no idea I would be writing this book of sermons based on the interpretations in that book.

But in the mystery of things, something was apparently at work in my unconscious that would lead to both the book and this sermon—and to the amazing appropriateness (considering the book on Mark) of the title "Hidden Easter."

As for my memories of finding Easter eggs within tall, fresh clumps of grass, I can still testify to their accuracy. Mark Twain once said he had a very good memory because he could even remember things that hadn't happened. But I recall very clearly the excitement I felt on Easter morning when I was six or seven years old and my parents would hide colored eggs in the yard for me and my little sister to find. Always there would be dozens of tall bunches of grass—probably a different kind of grass from the ordinary Bluegrass in which the yard was generally sown—that had taken a sudden leap forward while the rest of the grass was still dormant after the winter snows. And my parents knew that placing the eggs in those clumps would both disguise them and help us to find them more easily.

While I cannot say for certain how my mind was working on the day when I made the entry in my notebook, I imagine I had made some connection between this apparently abortive ending in Mark, which tends to hide the mystery the Gospel has tended so ferociously until these final sentences, and the brightly colored eggs I often discovered in the plainness of the tall grass. I am not sure how I planned to get from that beginning into a meaningful sermon—perhaps I was never able to figure it out and so never employed the introduction—but now I think I see a wonderful connection. It is part of the mystery—and the blessing—of Mark's stupendous Gospel.

The fact that many readers have been disappointed to think that the Gospel of Mark ends with chapter 16, verse 8, is underlined, I think, by the fact that some editors of the early manuscript found it incumbent on themselves to add a list of Jesus' post-resurrection appearances and thus bring it into harmony with the other Gospels, each of which narrated several marvelous stories about Jesus after his victory over death.

The first appearance in this short list is to Mary Magdalene, who, the editor informs us, had seven demons cast out of her by Jesus—a fact Mark has not bothered to tell us on at least one if not two earlier occasions on which Mary was mentioned but which is noted by Luke in Luke 8:2.

Then, says the editor, he appeared to two disciples "as they were walking into the country"—obviously the disciples from Emmaus whom we meet also in Matthew 16:12-13 and John 20:19-23 and much more fully and colorfully in Luke 24:13-35.

And finally, we are informed, Jesus appeared to the eleven disciples (*sans* Judas) as they sat "at the table," and upbraided them for "their lack of faith and stubbornness" (Mark 16:14). Having chided the disciples, Jesus then proceeded to dispatch them to "proclaim the good news to the whole creation"—obviously a sketchy version of the so-called Great Commission recorded at the end of the Gospel of Matthew.

But this whole performance by the unknown redactor is very limp and lame after the rest of Mark's Gospel—mere fish bones without any flesh on them. So it was quite easy, even before we had the advantage of computers with their formidable linguistic analyses, for some scholars to say, "Wait a minute, this isn't like Mark at all. It is bound to be an addition to the text by a manuscript copyist who didn't want the Gospel to end so bluntly, with the young man's announcement to the three

women, Mary Magdalene, Mary the mother of James, and Salome, that Jesus had been raised and they were to go back and
tell the others, and then their utter fecklessness in not telling
because they were gripped by "terror and amazement."

I know that most preachers avoid the Markan text on
Easter Sunday because it is so meatless, so lacking in the juicy
narrative of the other Gospels when they get to the point where
the authors can rub their hands and gloat over Jesus' reappear-
ance. I expect that if I surveyed my own Easter preaching across
the years, I would find that I too seldom preached from Mark
on Christianity's day of days.

But now I find Mark's abbreviated ending quite meaningful
and fulfilling because it requires me to go back into the earlier
pages of his Gospel to examine the two or possibly three places
where I believe we have already been given resurrection stories—namely, the calming-of-the-sea events in Mark 4:35-41
and Mark 6:45-52 and the transfiguration narrative in Mark
9:2-8—and I feel a *frisson* of excitement at these remarkable
demonstrations of the real meaning and power of Jesus' transcendence.

I have spoken earlier of the calming-of-the-sea stories and
the evidence that they are intended as portraits of the risen
Christ's coming to the Christian community whenever it has
been in any kind of difficulty, particularly when it has been in
danger of perishing. I believe this is the reason for Mark's treating the resurrection of Jesus as he did. He wanted his readers
to know that Christ is with us all the time, especially when we
are in trouble. He could have given us an account similar to
those in the other Gospels, but chose not to because he wished
to underline the spiritual, transcendent nature of Christ's pres-

ence. The sense of transcendence is actually enhanced by the understanding that it is not limited to a particular moment in time but is there at all times and in all places.

I find this much more comforting in my daily affairs—and trust that others do as well—than the knowledge that Jesus was raised up, period. He wasn't just raised up, period; he was raised up, he transcended mortality and other human problems for a purpose, to be with us whenever we undergo unusual stress and danger.

I have an old friend, Professor Wayne Pipkin, whom I met years ago when I was speaking at Baylor University for several days. Wayne was a young professor of religion there, and we hit it off instantly as persons of similar temperaments and with a similar commitment to Christ. One of my greatest joys that week was the opportunity to be in Wayne's home a few blocks off the campus. It was a neat little brick house erected on university property, and Wayne's wife Arlene had put many warm and beautiful touches into it as it was being built. She and Wayne had two darling little girls who were still preschoolers when I met them.

Wayne had been at Baylor for three years, and, according to the rules of the university, would either be asked to leave or be voted another three-year probation period or full tenure. If given another three years of probation, he would be considered again at the end of that period, and, if he failed to receive tenure then, would not be recommended for continuance on the faculty.

There was absolutely no doubt in my mind that Wayne would receive full tenure immediately, for he was a very popular and creative teacher, was enthusiastic about the school and its

programs, and had done enough publishing to warrant acceptance in the academic community.

But I did not reckon on two things. One was the amount
of jealousy some professors felt toward Wayne because of the
fine reviews he got from students. We would like to think such
jealousies do not exist in academia, but unfortunately they do.
The other thing was that Wayne wore a rather luxurious black
beard. Again, it was not something that should have affected
his vote for tenure. But this was in the 1970s, and Baylor was
a conservative institution. Most of its constituents were Southern Baptist, and Southern Baptist ministers, most people
thought, were supposed to be clean shaven.

Sadly, Wayne was turned down for further appointment.

He was crestfallen when he called to tell me the news. His
whole future had come tumbling down. He and his family
would have to leave the beautiful home they'd helped to design.
He would have to begin the tenure process again at another
school. Moreover, the news came so late in the academic year
that it would be all but impossible to find another situation before the following year, so Wayne and his family were moving
to Columbus, Ohio, to live with Arlene's family.

Later, in a book called *Christian Meditation*, Wayne related
the story of this great disappointment and how it affected him
and his family. He was depressed about the failure of his hopes
at Baylor and the slowness with which other work was becoming available, and wondered how he could continue to support
his wife and children. Everything looked very bleak.

One day he was thinking about the prayer practice of
Teresa of Avila, the great mystic who allowed her imagination
to become part of her prayer experience. Wanting to let his

imagination become a part of his own healing, Wayne did a simple little prayer exercise in which he mentally placed himself in a particular place and then waited to have some kind of word from God. Trying to relax, he imagined a place he had loved since attending seminary, the rocky seacoast of New England. He imagined that it was a sunny day and he was walking along the high shoreline and looking down at the sea. Then he climbed down the bluff and continued along the rocky beach. As he walked, he saw sunlight glinting on a bottle that was washing in and out with the waves. Believing there might be an important message for him in the bottle, he fished out the bottle.

There was indeed a message in the bottle, but he found it very disappointing. It said in Latin—which as a professor of church history he understood very well—*HODIE CHRISTUS NATUS EST.* "Today Christ is born." That was all. Nothing else. Nothing about his jobless situation. Nothing about the dashing of his vocational hopes at Baylor. Nothing about where the road was going to lead him in the future.

He felt dejected, he said. Here he was prepared for some extremely relevant message that would instantly renew his spirit, and all he received was an old phrase from some medieval hymn, *HODIE CHRISTUS NATUS EST.* Of course he knew Christ was born. He was a professor of church history. If Christ hadn't been born, he wouldn't even be a professor and wouldn't be in the mess he was in.

Then, he said, it hit him! Not relevant? It was the most relevant message in the world! Christ was born! It made all the difference in everything—even his unfortunate fiscal condition, his depression, his future.

That message about Christ's birth, he wrote, "was not an idle affirmation of faith. Rather, it was a rekindling of faith down at the very roots of my being. In the midst of apparent insecurity, I discovered an insight into lasting security!"[1]

Suddenly Wayne felt like singing. Christ is born! Christ the Savior! God manifest in our midst!

Nothing could have been *more* relevant!

I realize this is an Easter sermon, about Christ's resurrection, and not a Christmas sermon, about his birth. But in Mark's eyes it was pretty much one and the same: *born, died, was raised up,* they all spelled God's intervention in the human condition. It was the *fact* of Christ that made all the difference. As God manifesting the divine nature in the midst of our human dilemmas, he assured us of heavenly participation in all our woes and needs.

Wayne's affairs soon picked up. He got a teaching post in the Baptist Theological Seminary in Rüschlikon, Switzerland, and is still there lecturing, publishing books, and spreading the good news of Christ's birth, death, and resurrection. But I am confident that, even if he had not found a new position, and had been forced to work as a clerk in a store or a laborer on a farm, Wayne would have lived in transcendence of the mere facts of his existence.

He had discovered what the Gnostics of the early church discovered, that material things don't matter all that much in life, it is the spirit that counts; and when one knows that, when one is in touch with the living spirit of Christ in our midst, no storms can sink us or destroy our faith.

The women did well to run away and tell no one what had happened at Jesus' tomb, for they had had confirmed to them

---

1. H. Wayne Pipkin, *Christian Meditation: Its Art and Practice* (Hawthorn Books, 1977), p. 57.

what Mary Magdalene, at least, already knew when she anointed his head with oil, the mystery that St. Paul would one day put in these words: "God was in Christ reconciling the world to himself."[2]

Perhaps the last word of the sermon ought to be St. Paul's, for he gave a very effective summary of what Mark was trying to say, that

> We have this treasure in clay jars, so that it may be made clear that this extraordinary power belongs to God and does not come from us. We are afflicted in every way, but not crushed; perplexed, but not driven to despair; persecuted, but not forsaken; struck down, but not destroyed; always carrying in the body the death of Jesus, so that the life of Jesus may also be made visible in our bodies. For while we live, we are always being given up to death for Jesus' sake, so that the life of Jesus may be made visible in our mortal flesh.[3]

Isn't that what Mark was saying all along?

2. 2 Corinthians 5:19, KJV.
3. 2 Corinthians 4:7-11.

Breinigsville, PA USA
14 October 2010
247304BV00001B/6/P